Instructor's Manual
for
Christensen

Experimental Methodology

Instructor's Manual for Christensen **Experimental Methodology**

Fifth Edition

Prepared by

Larry B. Christensen
Texas A & M University

Cheryl Frenck
University de Provence

Allyn and Bacon
Boston London Toronto Sydney Tokyo Singapore

A Division of Simon & Schuster, Inc.
160 Gould Street
Needham Heights, Massachusetts 02194

ISBN 0-205-12727-4

Printed in the United States of America

10 9 8 7 6 5 4 3 2 1 95 94 93 92 91 90

CONTENTS

Instructor's Manual for Christensen

Experimental Methodology

Chapter 1

What is Science?

Multiple Choice

1. Tenacity refers to all of the following except:

   (a) a means of acquiring knowledge
   (b) persistence of a superstition
   * (c) intuitive inclination
   (d) quality or state holding fast

2. Empiricism is:

   * (a) an unscientific approach for attaining knowledge
   (b) knowledge based on specific scientific techniques
   (c) knowledge acquired through reasoning
   (d) knowledge acquired from a reliable source

3. Which of the following approaches assumes that valid knowledge is acquired if the correct reasoning process is used?

   (a) empiricism
   (b) intuition
   * (c) rationalism
   (d) tenacity

4. All of the following are advantages of the scientific method except:

   (a) the scientific method relies on data obtained through empirical observation
   (b) the scientific method uses a systematic logic of inquiry
   (c) the scientific method uses observations which are independent of bias
   * (d) replication of results is often easy when using the scientific method

5. Which of the following is the least acceptable means of acquiring knowledge?

   (a) rationalism
   * (b) tenacity
   (c) empiricism
   (d) authority
   (e) science

6. The scientific method specifies that we obtain observations through a specific and systematic logic of inquiry. These observations must be independent of opinion, bias, and prejudice. In other words, scientific observations must be:

(a) personal
(b) rational
* (c) objective
(d) intuitive
(e) all of the above

7. What is perhaps the single most important element in the scientific method?

(a) operational definition
(b) sample size
* (c) control
(d) prediction
(e) generalization

8. Science can best be described as:

(a) a body of knowledge
* (b) a logic of inquiry
(c) a rational thought process
(d) empirical data

9. Control implies:

(a) constancy
(b) directing antecedent conditions
(c) comparison
* (d) all of the above

10. Scientific understanding requires which of the following objectives?

(a) description, explanation, prediction, replication
(b) operational definition, control, replication, description
* (c) description, prediction, control, explanation
(d) control, description, operational definition, explanation
(e) replication, operational definition, prediction, control

11. Operationism refers to:

* (a) defining terms by the methods used to attain them
(b) defining the reason for a study
(c) defining the operations that the researcher wants to study
(d) defining the extraneous factors in a study

12. When one defines terms by the steps used to measure them, this person is incorporating the principle of

* (a) operational definition
(b) control
(c) description
(d) explanation

13. Rationalism refers to acquisition of knowledge by means of:

(a) a specific scientific technique
* (b) reasoning
(c) subjective analysis
(d) conferring with experts

14. Control means:

(a) comparison groups
(b) eliminating or holding extraneous variables constant
(c) guidance or directing to produce an exact change or specific behavior
* (d) all of the above

15. To which of the following does control <u>not</u> refer?

(a) a check or verification in terms of a comparison
* (b) being able to select subjects
(c) keeping conditions constant
(d) directing in the sense of producing an exact change

16. Operational definitions have been criticized because:

(a) they do not allow for total control of extraneous variables
* (b) they lead to a multiplication of concepts
(c) their demands are not strict enough
(d) they hinder scientific communication
(e) they are difficult to use

17. Defining terms by the procedures used to measure them refers to:

(a) the scientific method
(b) technique
(c) empiricism
* (d) operationalism
(e) control

18. Replication can be achieved by making:

(a) intrasubject observations
(b) intersubject observations
(c) intergroup observations
* (d) all of the above

19. The reproducibility of observations can be investigated by making intergroup, intersubject, or intrasubject observations. Intersubject observations involve

(a) attempting to duplicate the results with the same subjects on different occasions
* (b) assessing the reliability of observations on other individual subjects
(c) attempting to duplicate the results on another group of subjects
(d) none of the above

20. What axiom must the scientist accept?

(a) nature is predictable
(b) some things in nature are unpredictable
* (c) there is uniformity in nature
(d) there are few lawful relations in nature

21. Determinism is the belief that

(a) behavior is stable and invariant
(b) behavior is predetermined by variables beyond one's control
* (c) behavior is caused by specific events
(d) behavior has no causes; it is random
(e) behavior has multiple causes

22. Objective observation is

(a) that which depends on opinion
(b) an important aspect of rationalism
* (c) that which precludes bias or prejudice
(d) not necessary when employing the scientific method

23. Description is the first objective of science. In the process of describing the phenomenon, which of the following is not a requirement?

(a) portray the phenomenon accurately
(b) identify the existing variables
* (c) identify antecedent conditions that result in the occurrence of the phenomenon
(d) determine the degree to which the variables exist

24. Control is an important concept in the proper implementation of the scientific method. Boring notes that the word control has three meanings. These include all of the following <u>except</u>

* (a) to influence or control behavior
(b) elimination of the influence of extraneous variables
(c) a comparison group
(d) manipulation of antecedent conditions to produce a change in behavior

25. Which of the following is not one of the three most important characteristics of science?

(a) replication
* (b) generalizability
(c) control
(d) operational definition

26. Which of the following is false about scientific techniques?

(a) they vary within the field of psychology
(b) they vary with the nature of the subject matter
* (c) they are constant within the field of psychology
(d) they vary with the stage of inquiry
(e) they are used when implementing the scientific method

27. Acquiring knowledge from a respected source is an example of the method of

(a) empiricism
(b) rationalism
* (c) authority
(d) tenacity

28. The various disciplines that utilize the scientific method for generating data make use of a wide variety of techniques. These techniques vary according to the

(a) nature of the specific problem
(b) stage of inquiry
(c) nature of the subject matter
* (d) a and c
(e) all of the above

29. Which of the following describe the role theory plays in the scientific process?

(a) accumulate scientific facts
(b) suggest new ideas and direct additional research
(c) integrate and summarize scientific facts
* (d) b and c
(e) all of the above

30. Intrasubject observation consists of:

(a) attempting to duplicate the results on another group of subjects
* (b) attempting to duplicate the results with the same set of subjects
(c) assessing the reliability of observations on other individual subjects
(d) attempting to duplicate the results on a different set of subjects on the same occasion

31. Scientific understanding requires all of the following objectives except:

(a) prediction
(b) explanation
(c) description
* (d) operationism
(e) control

32. The concepts of control, replication, and operationism differentiate the scientific approach from:

(a) empiricism
(b) rationalism
(c) intuition
* (d) all of the above

33. If an investigator were to define aggression in terms of the frequency and intensity of shock administered to another person, he or she would have used:

(a) a scientific technique
* (b) an operational definition
(c) a method of inquiry
(d) a rationalism

34. Which method of acquiring knowledge represents religious doctrines

(a) tenacity
* (b) authority
(c) rationalism
(d) empiricism
(e) none of the above

35. Mere exposure refers to

(a) the results of an experiment focusing on the environment
(b) having received minimal exposure to research
* (c) a process involved in attitude formation
(d) developing a positive attitude toward research once exposed to it

36. Tenacity, as a method of acquiring information, has the following limitation(s)

(a) the knowledge may be inaccurate
(b) you may persist in believing the knowledge
(c) it does not provide a mechanism for correcting erroneous beliefs
* (d) both a and c

37. Rationalism, as a method of acquiring information, has the following limitation(s)

(a) the knowledge may be inaccurate
(b) the knowledge may not correspond to reality
(c) this method is used only within philosophy
* (d) both a and b

<u>Fill in the Blank</u>

1. The _____________ approach to the acquisition of knowledge should not be confused with information from experts since experts usually impart scientific knowledge.
(authority)

2. Reasoning is a vital element in the scientific process; it is used to formulate or arrive at _________________.
(hypothesis)

3. ____________________ is the act or process of coming to direct knowledge or certainty without reasoning or inferring.
(Intuition)

4. ________________ is the knowledge acquired through reasoning.
(Rationalism)

5. ____________ is acceptance of information because it is attained from a highly respected source.
(Authority)

6. Knowledge acquired through ______________ is referred to as empiricism.
(Experience)

7. In many experiments, ____________ must be conducted with the subjects to assess their reaction to the experiment and to eliminate any undesirable influence the experiment may have created.
(debriefing or postinterviews)

8. After data collection and statistical analysis is completed, the experimenters must interpret results and specify their meaning; this occurs in the __________ phase of the scientific method.
(hypothesis testing)

9. Science represents a method or _____________ to be followed in solving problems and thus obtaining a body of knowledge.
(logic of inquiry)

10. _____________ is an absolutely essential process in science because the cause of an effect could not be isolated without it.
(Control)

11. _____________ observations involves attempting to duplicate the results of a study on another group of subjects.
(Intergroup)

12. Only through ______________ can we place any confidence in the fact that the results of our studies are valid and reliable.
(replication)

13. _____________ is the most important element in the scientific method.
(control)

14. The objective of science concerned with the ability to anticipate the occurrence of an event is _________________.
(prediction)

15. The ultimate objective of science is to understand the world around us. Scientific understanding requires four specific objectives: _____________, ____________, ________________, ___________.
(description, prediction, explanation, control)

16. Implicit in the assumption of uniformity in nature is the concept of ___________ the belief that there are causes, or determinants, of behavior.
(determinism)

17. The axiom that the scientist must accept is that there is __________ in nature.
(uniformity)

18. __________ as a method of acquiring knowledge represents religious doctrines.
(Authority)

19. Knowledge that is acquired through the __________ __________ is the only type that is scientific knowledge.
(scientific method)

20. Defining terms by the procedures used to measure them is referred to as __________.
(operationalism)

21. __________ is the least acceptable means of acquiring knowledge.
(Tenacity)

22. __________refers to the manipulation of the conditions that determine a phenomenon.
(Control)

23. The acquisition of scientific knowledge typically begins with __________ .
(description)

24. __________ varies with the nature of the scientific problem, the subject matter, and the stage of the investigation.
(Technique)

25. __________ is very important in an experiment because it enables researchers to determine the causes of their observation.
(Control)

26. Replication, control, and operational definitions are characteristics of __________ .
(science)

True or False

1. The tenacity approach of acquiring knowledge seems to boil down to the acquisition and persistence of superstitions.
(True)

2. Intuition is the act or process of coming to direct knowledge or certainty through reasoning or inferring.
(False)

3. In science, empiricism refers to the personal experience of the event.
(False)

4. Authority as a method of acquiring knowledge is a cornerstone of science.
(False)

5. If the results of a given study are not replicated in a second study, this means that the first study was undoubtedly poorly run.
(False)

6. Psychologists use a logic of inquiry that is the same as other sciences.
(True)

7. Establishing proper controls over extraneous variables is an important step in conducting an experiment.
(True)

8. The communication of research results most frequently takes place at annual conventions.
(False)

9. The first step in the scientific process involves conducting a literature review and formulating the research problem.
(True)

10. The three most important characteristics of science include explanation, prediction and control.
(False)

11. Operationalism of terms is necessary to eliminate confusion in communication.
(True)

12. The sequence of activities specified in the five steps of the research process are usually not followed.
(True)

13. One must take experimenter and setting differences into consideration when interpreting a study that has failed to replicate prior results.
(True)

14. Many researchers are committed to conducting replication research.
(False)

15. As a procedural step, hypothesis testing follows the actual conduct of the experiment.
(True)

16. Knowledge acquired through experience is called empiricism.
(True)

17. Rationalism is the most acceptable non-scientific means of acquiring knowledge.
(False)

18. Psychology uses a variety of different techniques in applying the basic scientific method.
(True)

19. Reliability can be determined by making intergroup, intersubject, or intrasubject observations.
(True)

20. The acceptance of information acquired through our perceptions is an example of rationalism.
(False)

21. The basic assumption underlying science is that uniformity in nature must exist in order to develop facts, theories, and laws.
(True)

22. Science has certain objectives that it strives to achieve in attempting to reach the goal of understanding the world around us. These objectives include description, prediction, explanation and control.
(True)

23. The scientist must fully accept results of prior studies.
(False)

24. Serendipity, i.e. coming across a result one was not looking for, can lead to important discoveries in science.
(True)

25. Theories provide science with many facts.
(False)

Chapter 2

Ethics

Multiple Choice

1. Why is ethics an issue in psychological research?

   (a) Because subjects have a right to know
   (b) Because at times subjects rights interfere with researchers rights as people
   * (c) Because it is often necessary for research to impinge upon individual's rights
   (d) Because many law suits have been filed
   (e) Because subjects need to be educated about psychology

2. Which of the following is not an area of ethical concern for the social scientist:

   (a) the relationship between society and science
   * (b) potential for "real life" application of the results
   (c) professional issues
   (d) treatment of subjects

3. The only justification for deliberately altering scientific data is:

   (a) legitimate moral and social concerns
   (b) to better illustrate the test of the hypothesis, and then only if the alteration is in the direction of general trend of the results.
   (c) to obtain funding for future, socially valuable research
   (d) a and b but not c
   * (e) none of the above, it is always unjustified

4. Which of the following would not be considered at least a "minimal risk" to the human research subject:

   (a) exposure to psychologically stressful conditions
   (b) exposure to guilt inducing conditions
   (c) experiments using deception
   (d) b and c
   * (e) all would be considered at least "minimal risk"

5. The ethical acceptability of any study must always reside with:

   (a) the ethics committees
   (b) the investigator's colleagues
   * (c) the investigator
   (d) an institutional review board

6. When an investigator uses assistants, collaborators, students, employees, etc., to help conduct research, the final responsibility for the decision to conduct a study falls upon:

* (a) everyone involved
(b) an ethics committee
(c) the institutional review board
(d) the investigator

7. In a study involving more than one investigator:

(a) addition of investigators dilutes responsibility from the main investigator
(b) students and assistants are not the responsibility of the principle investigator
(c) ethics is not a great concern because the study is planned between investigators
(d) only the principal investigator is held responsible for the ethics
* (e) each coprincipal investigator is equally responsible for the ethical conduct of the study

8. When using deception in a study, which of the following is not required of the investigator?

(a) consideration of alternative procedures
* (b) informed consent
(c) consideration of whether deception is justified given the potential value of the study
(d) a sufficient explanation of the study

9. One of the difficulties with debriefing subjects is:

(a) it may anger or disillusion the subject
(b) the subject is no longer naive and will be less acceptable for future research
(c) the subject may believe that the debriefing is a deception.
* (d) a and c
(e) all of the above

10. Subjects should not be debriefed when:

(a) they are likely to file a complaint with the APA
(b) they may divulge vital information about the experiment to other potential subjects
(c) they could not easily understand the purpose of the study
* (d) the debriefing itself might cause them stress
(e) none of the above; subjects must always be debriefed

11. Some psychologists have argued against acceptance of APA's ethical guidelines because:

* (a) to be considered "minimal risk" the experimental manipulations will have to be relatively mild and less likely to elicit subject motivation.
(b) few subjects have really been harmed by their participation resulting from the subject's participation.
(c) it involves more meticulous experimental design

12. Gergen's position on the APA ethical guidelines is that:

* (a) scientists should determine the effects of each principle before making them ethical standards to be followed
(b) the guidelines will be helpful because they allow for more powerful manipulations
(c) the principles would be helpful to the professional and create an enhancement of knowledge
(d) the principles will help protect the rights of human beings

13. Which of the following is not true with regard to the use of deception?

(a) deception has been steadily increasing in the past thirty years
(b) deception is very common in social psychology
(c) deception is very common in personality research
* (d) deception has little or no potential for harmful effects

14. According to Holmes the two goals of debriefing are __________ and __________.

(a) deception; sensitizing
(b) dehoaxing; sensitizing
* (c) dehoaxing; desensitizing
(d) deceiving; desensitizing

15. Which of the following is true with regard to debriefing:

(a) one should always use debriefing
(b) one should debrief only under special circumstances
* (c) one should eliminate debriefing in certain circumstances
(d) one should debrief only when the subject knows he/she has been deceived

16. If a subject has been made aware of some undesirable feature of themself, the debriefing procedure to use would be:

(a) sensitization
* (b) desensitization
(c) dehoaxing
(d) do not debrief in this circumstance

17. According to the studies cited in the text which of the following are the most strict in their interpretation of human research ethics?

* (a) researchers
(b) ethics committees
(c) law professors
(d) research participants

18. Studies investigating the perceptions of research participants from the subject pool reveal that they generally view their experience as:

(a) negative but usually coercive
* (b) positive but sometimes coercive
(c) negative but noncoercive
(d) positive and noncoercive

19. The major ethical dilemma facing the scientific investigator concerns:

(a) the importance of the research
(b) violation of subject's rights
* (c) the tradeoff between possible contributions of a study vs. cost to the subject
(d) deception

20. Under which of the following conditions may debriefing not be necessary?

(a) when it was not stipulated by ethical principles
(b) when the study is of an innocuous nature
(c) when the subject does not request it
(d) when it would bias the outcome of the study
* (e) when the treatment condition falls within the subject's range of ordinary every day experiences

21. Ethical concerns in the social and behavioral sciences consist of:

(a) professional issues
(b) treatment of subjects
(c) relationship between society and science
* (d) all of the above

22. In studies where deception is used, __________ is not required however __________ should take place at some point.

* (a) informed consent, debriefing
  (b) desensitizing, informed consent
  (c) debriefing, payment of subjects
  (d) payment of subjects, informed consent

23. Which of the following determines the issues to be investigated by researchers?

  (a) federal government
  (b) society
  (c) the researchers
* (d) all of the above

24. Ethics involved in professional issues mostly concern:

* (a) honesty in reporting research results
  (b) proper treatment of subjects
  (c) use of deception
  (d) freedom of choice

25. Consideration of __________ is the first and most fundamental issue to be confronted by the scientist.

  (a) the use of deception
  (b) the importance of the proposed study
  (c) informed consent
* (d) treatment of subjects
  (e) debriefing procedures

26. When did ethical issues become a dominant concern for scientists:

  (a) 1930's
  (b) mid 1940's
  (c) mid 1950's
* (d) mid 1960's

27. Researchers should resolve the ethical dilemma by:

  (a) consulting colleagues
  (b) consulting ethics committees
* (c) weighing possible benefits against costs
  (e) following APA ethical guidelines

28. According to the APA ethical guidelines which of the following conditions may make the use of deception more acceptable?

(a) subjects are allowed to withdraw from the study at any time
(b) investigator takes full responsibility for removing any stressful aftereffects
(c) the study is of great importance and cannot be carried out without using deception
* (d) all of the above

29. One of the most controversial ethical issues surrounding the use of subject pools in psychology departments concerns:

(a) deception
(b) debriefing
(c) generalizability
(d) informed consent
* (e) coercion

30. Resnick and Schwartz found that subjects provided with complete informed consent:

(a) were usually more cooperative
(b) were usually less cooperative
(c) lost interest in the study
(d) performed differently than less informed subjects
* (e) all of the above except (a)

31. At least one study has revealed that informing participants of their freedom to withdraw resulted in:

* (a) a reduction in the effect of the experimental treatment.
(b) a rapid decline of voluntary participation
(c) an increase in voluntary participation
(d) increased dissatisfaction with the subjects' participation in the study

32. When an animal is no longer required for a study the experimenter should:

(a) euthanize the animal immediately
* (b) consider transferring it to a colleague who could use them
(c) return it to the distributor
(d) retain it for breeding purposes

33. Which of the following are possible reasons why a scientists may engage in fraudulent activity.

(a) the publish or parish phenomenon
(b) stress from competing in a competitive research environment
(c) a personality defect
* (d) all of the above

34. Safeguards against scientific fraud include

(a) the results of scientific experiments are open to inspection by other scientists
(b) every study is peer reviewed prior to publication
(c) replication
* (d) all of the above

35. Deception studies are typically viewed as being more unacceptable if they are conducted to investigate

(a) private behaviors
(b) behavior which involves harming another
(c) sexual behavior
(d) any type of deception
* (e) all of the above except d

36. The regulations regarding the promotion and care of research animal's psychological health focus on issues such as

(a) increasing cage size
(b) exercise for the animals
(c) enrichment of nonhuman primate's environment
(d) allowing animals to forage for food
* (e) all of the above

<u>Fill in the Blank</u>

1. Ethics became a dominant concern during the decade of the ___________.
(1960's)

2. The final decision about the ethical responsibility and merit of an experiment lies with ______________.
(the experimenter)

3. APA stands for _______.
(American Psychological Association)

4. The cost and risks to the participants must be weighed against a study's __________.
(potential benefits)

5. According to the studies cited in the text, __________ are usually strictest in their interpretation of human research ethics.
(researchers)

6. Research participants drawn from subject pools generally view their experience as positive but __________.
(coercive)

7. Informing the subject about the purpose and nature of the experiment once his participation is ended is called __________.
(debriefing)

8. The APA ethics committee listed __________ principles for research with humans.
(ten)

9. The use of __________ in research increased between 1948 and the 1970s and is difficult to avoid in some studies.
(deception)

10. Eliminating any undesirable influence that the experiment may have had on a subject is called __________.
(desensitizing)

11. Dehoaxing and desensitizing are both part of the ________ process.
(debriefing)

12. __________ refers to debriefing participants about any deception that was used in the experiment.
(dehoaxing)

13. According to the text, deception appears to have a more negative effect on __________ than it does on the _________.
(researchers; participants)

14. If subjects are informed of the exact nature of an experiment prior to participating in it, the __________ validity of the study may be jeopardized.
(external)

15. According to studies cited in the text, most subjects view the subject pool __________.
(positively)

16. Informing subjects that they may be deceived, but not of the exact nature of the deception __________ alter results.
(does not)

17. An animal should be __________ as soon as possible following participation in an experiment requiring severe distress or unalleviated pain.
(euthanized)

18. Experimenters should use __________ procedures in lieu of aversive treatments whenever possible.
(appetitive)

True or False

1. Societal values are of no concern to the truly objective social scientist.
(false)

2. Government spending, at least partially, dictates research topics in the social sciences.
(true)

3. In its 1982 report on ethical principles the APA suggested that animal subjects should be granted the same rights as their human counterparts.
(false)

4. When considering the pros and cons of the ethical dilemma, primary consideration must be given to the potential gains from conducting the experiment.
(false)

5. Ethical issues became a dominant concern in the mid 1950's.
(false)

6. Informing subjects of the purpose of an experiment prior to conducting it may create a lack of external validity.
(true)

7. In making difficult ethical decision the APA suggests that a researcher seek the opinions of others.
(true)

8. It is not appropriate to conclude that research cannot be conducted if it imposes some risk to the participant.
(true)

9. The investigator is ultimately responsible for the ethical acceptability of a study.
(true)

10. According to studies cited in the text, most students view the subject pool negatively.
(false)

11. A psychology professor requires his students to participate in at least 3 of his own studies per semester or forfeit one letter grade. According to APA guidelines this would qualify as unethical coercion.
(true)

12. There are some situations in which the subjects should not be debriefed.
(true)

13. Research data is protected by the same laws of confidentiality as the information obtained in therapy.
(false)

14. Dehoaxing refers to debriefing subjects about their behaviors.
(false)

15. Desensitizing refers to an attempt to eliminate any undesirable influence that the experiment may have had on the subject.
(true)

16. Deception has been steadily increasing in the past thirty years.
(true)

17. According to studies cited in the test, there is little difference in the outcome of research where subjects are informed about the purpose of the study.
(false)

18. Once a subject has agreed to participate in a study the actual data from that subject belongs to the researcher and may be used in any way the researcher deems appropriate.
(false)

19. Research suggests that in most cases even complete informed consent has little effect on a subject's experimental performance.
(false)

20. Informing subjects that they are free to withdraw at anytime without penalty can influence the outcome of some experiments.
(true)

Chapter 3

Descriptive Research Approaches

Multiple Choice

1. The descriptive research approach has as it's goal(s):

   (a) identify variables that exist in a given situation
   (b) determine a cause-and-effect relationship
   (c) description of the relationship that exists between the identified variables
   * (d) a and c
   (e) all of the above

2. Participant observation and naturalistic observation are both

   a. good techniques to use when a correctional study would be unethical
   b. experimental techniques used with observational data
   * c. purely descriptive
   d. suitable for use in the laboratory as well as in the field

3. The primary advantage of using the descriptive technique of secondary records is that they are not subject to the potentially biasing

   (a) selective survival effect
   (b) selective deposit effect
   * (c) reactivity effect
   (d) none of the above are advantages

4. Although the participant observation technique allows a researcher to examine a situation that might otherwise be closed to investigation, it also involves the significant risk of introducing various biases into the description. Such biases include

   (a) loss of objectivity
   (b) personal attitudes
   (c) reactivity effect
   * (d) a and b
   (e) b and c

5. Naturalistic observation accomplishes all of the following except:

(a) unobtrusive collection of data
* (b) isolating causes of behavior
(c) generating hypotheses
(d) description of behavior

6. A study that attempts to describe the degree of relationship that exists between two measured variables.

(a) survey
* (b) correlational study
(c) longitudinal study
(d) ex post facto study

7. Descriptive research approaches are so named because

a. they describe causal relationships between variables
b. they describe the manipulation of variables
c. they describe how behavior can be controlled
* d. they describe events in their natural state

8. A disadvantage of the survey is that:

(a) they are simple to administer
(b) they reduce sampling error
* (c) they are necessarily short in length
(d) they require no time limit
(e) they answer the question "how many?"

9. Which of the following is true about naturalistic observation?

(a) several different approaches can be used
(b) the investigator is obtrusively involved
(c) causality can be determined
* (d) observations are made on specific aspects of behavior
(e) antecedent determinants of behavior can be identified

10. Which of the following is <u>not</u> a disadvantage of the survey approach?

(a) sampling error exists in the survey
(b) time constraints exist in the survey
* (c) surveys answer questions such as "how many"
(d) there are constraints in the length of the survey

11. A developmental field study that measures the same characteristics in representative samples of individuals at different age levels is called a

(a) ex post facto study
(b) longitudinal study
(c) correlational study
* (d) cross-sectional study

12. The age-cohort effect is associated with which of the following descriptive research approaches?

(a) naturalistic observation
* (b) longitudinal and cross-sectional studies
(c) correlational studies
(d) surveys
(e) all of the above

13. Suppose a researcher assigned pregnant women to one of two treatment groups based on whether or not they smoked, and than measured the birth weights of their babies. This is

(a) a true experiment
* (b) an ex post facto study
(c) a case study
(d) an unethical study

14. Ex post facto studies differ from other descriptive studies in that

(a) many of them closely resemble an experiment
(b) some combine ex post facto and the experimental approach in a single design
(c) the variables being manipulated are under the experimenter's control
* (d) a and b
(e) b and c

15. Most studies using secondary records have little potential for a reactivity effect because

(a) only certain types of data are initially recorded
(b) the data are typically recorded within the context of a research study
(c) only certain types of data are selected to be retained
* (d) the data are typically recorded outside the context of a research study

16. The effect of sex and drug dosage on fatigue represents a research question. Which variable(s) represent(s) an ex post facto variable(s)?

(a) fatigue
(b) sex and fatigue
* (c) sex
(d) drug dosage
(e) fatigue and drug dosage

17. Ex post facto studies resemble correlational studies in that the relationships obtained

(a) enables us to accomplish the goal of prediction
(b) allows us to infer causation
* (c) may have been produced by variables other than those investigated in the study
(d) none of the above

18. Meta analysis is a ___________ technique used to integrate and describe a large number of studies

(a) predictive
(b) correlational
(c) qualitative
* (d) quantitative

20. An ex post facto study is an example of:

(a) an experimental approach
* (b) a descriptive approach
(c) both descriptive and experimental approaches
(d) a study where the experimenter has control over the manipulated variable.

21. When the purpose of an inquiry is to find the degree of relationship which exists between two variables, which of the following is the most appropriate approach?

* (a) correlational study
(b) survey
(c) field study
(d) longitudinal study
(e) none of the above

22. Which of the following is true of naturalistic observation?

(a) it requires a relatively short length of time to complete
* (b) it is necessary to use this approach in situations in which one wants to study natural behavior
(c) causality is easily isolated
(d) the observer plays an active role in the recorded activity

23. In which type of approach does the investigator take two or more groups of subjects who already differ on a certain variable and observe differences in their behavior?

(a) experimental
(b) cross-sectional
(c) longitudinal
(d) naturalistic
* (e) ex post facto

24. A large group of adolescents are administered IQ tests over a period of eight years to describe growth in intelligence. What type of study is this?

(a) naturalistic observation
(b) field study
* (c) longitudinal
(d) cross sectional

25. Which of the following would be the best approach to use to study the development of language in children given that you have only two months to run your study?

(a) correlational
(b) case history
(c) longitudinal
* (d) cross-sectional

26. Cross sectional studies:

(a) study changes in individuals from a cross section of the population
(b) repeatedly measure the same characteristics in a single sample of people at selected time intervals
(c) measure changes across time in individuals of both sexes
* (d) measure the same characteristics in a representative sample of people at different age levels

27. An intensive description and analysis of a single individual, organization or event is a

* (a) case study
(b) naturalistic observation
(c) secondary record
(d) longitudinal study
(e) meta-analysis

28. The case study is valuable for

(a) obtaining a description of naturally occurring behavior
(b) identifying the degree of relationship that exists between variables
(c) developing ideas and hypotheses
(d) describing rare events
* (e) both c and d

29. The limitations of the case study include

(a) inability to identify causal relationships
(b) inability to describe rare events
(c) inability to generalize to other individuals or situations
(d) inability to generate hypotheses and ideas
* (e) both a and c

<u>Fill in the Blank</u>

1. The _________ _________ _________ is a technique that provides a description or picture of a particular situation, event or set of events.
(Descriptive research approach)

2. A descriptive research technique used for unobtrusively collecting data on naturally occurring behavior is ____________ ____________.
(naturalistic observation)

3. Any recorded observation, measure, or physical trace made by others are referred to as a ________ ___________.
(secondary record)

4. The term __________ refers to the potentially biasing effect that occurs as a result of knowing that one is part of a study or that the data being collected will be closely examined in the future.
(reactivity effect)

5. The main disadvantage of using secondary records is the problem of selective recording of data, or __________ __________.
(selective deposit)

6. Since someone must decide what records are to be maintained, __________refers to survival over time of only certain records.
(selective survival)

7. __________ __________involves the observation and recording of the behavior of others while at the same time actively participating in the interactional situation.
(participant observation)

8. A population includes all of the things, people or events that are the object of the investigation whereas the __________ includes any number of things, people or events less than the total population.
(sample)

9. The correlational approach enables us not only to describe a relationship between two variables but also __________ one variable from the knowledge of the other variable.
(predict)

10. The __________ study approach enables one to accomplish the goal of prediction, but not necessarily determine causation.
(correlational)

11. Although one may gain the power of prediction with the correlational approach, one may not infer ______________.
(causation)

12. Tunnell's three dimensions of naturalness are: _________, _________ and ____________.
(behavior; setting; treatment)

13. The ___________ study involves choosing a single group of subjects and measuring specified characteristics at selected time intervals.
(longitudinal)

14. The _____________ study identifies representative samples of individuals at specific age groups and documents the changes in the selected characteristics of subjects in these different age groups.
(cross-sectional)

15. Unobtrusive observation is a key element necessary in a(n) ___________ ___________ type of study.
(naturalistic observation)

16. A study that compares the effects of two or more variables where the variables being manipulated are not under experimenter's control is referred to as a/an ____________ study.
(ex post facto)

17. Glass (1976) introduced the term __________ __________ to describe a quantitative approach that could be used to integrate and describe the results of a large number of studies.
(meta analysis)

True or False

1. The primary characteristic of descriptive research methodology is that it provides an accurate description of a particular phenomenon.
(True)

2. Most studies using secondary records have a high potential for a reactivity effect since the data are typically recorded outside the context of a research study.
(False)

3. The descriptive research approach attempts to establish cause-and-effect relationships.
(False)

4. Naturalistic observation is conducted when an investigator wants to eliminate any artificial influence that might result from bringing the subject out of the natural environment.
(True)

5. A unique characteristic of naturalistic observation is its obtrusiveness.
(False)

6. Selective deposit and the reactivity effect are both disadvantages of using secondary records.
(False)

7. Primary records within our society include vital statistics such as birth records, marriages, and census data.
(False)

8. A correlational study seeks to determine the causal relationship that exists between two measured variables.
(False)

9. Gallup poll type of research identifies cause-effect relationships.
(False)

10. A major disadvantage of a survey is that it is time consuming.
(False)

11. One significant advantage of cross-sectional and longitudinal type studies is that they very often lead to similar results, and thus can be used interchangeably.
(False)

12. Sampling error arises in surveys because of random sampling techniques.
(False)

13. The correlational approach enables us to accomplish the goal of prediction.
(True)

14. Causation can usually be inferred from correlation.
(False)

15. A longitudinal study repeatedly measures the same characteristic at selected time intervals in different, representative samples of individuals.
(False)

16. Although both the longitudinal and cross-sectional studies are descriptive research approaches, it is possible to conduct an experimental longitudinal or cross-sectional study.
(True)

17. One disadvantage of longitudinal and cross-sectional studies is that they yield similar results, and therefore are redundant.
(False)

18. In an ex post facto study, the variables being manipulated are under the experimenter's control.
(False)

19. The process of self-selection inherent in an ex post facto study is a primary weakness.
(True)

20. The main advantage of an ex post facto study is that it controls for self-selection, thus weeding out variables that are not self-selected.
(False)

21. Two related characteristics of naturalistic observation are the unobtrusiveness of the observer and the lack of artificiality of the situation.
(True)

Chapter 4

Experimental Research Approaches

<u>Multiple Choice</u>

1. Observations which are free from impartiality and bias on the part of the investigator are said to be

   (a) empirical
   (b) controlled
   * (c) objective
   (d) all of the above

2. According to Zimney (1961), there are several rules that investigators should follow when making empirical observations in order to minimize recording and observation errors. Which of the following is not one of these rules?

   (a) accept the possibility that mistakes can occur
   (b) attempt to identify where the mistakes are likely to occur
   * (c) account for any errors in the statistical analysis of the data
   (d) avoid the errors by taking necessary steps.

3. In psychological experimentation, one of the most pressing problems facing the experimenter is _________, without which causation could not be identified.

   (a) defining the phenomenon
   * (b) control
   (c) holding all factors constant
   (d) accounting for internal processes

4. Which of the following is not true of the experimental approach?

   (a) control
   * (b) partiality
   (c) objectivity
   (d) variation and constancy of variation

5. The foremost advantage of the experimental approach is the control that can be exercised. Other advantages of this approach are purely pragmatic ones. Which of the following is not necessarily one of these advantages?

* (a) studies are conducted quickly
(b) results that last over time
(c) suggestions for new studies
(d) suggestions for solutions to practical problems

6. There have been several criticisms leveled against the experimental approach. The most frequent and severe criticism is the

(a) time required to plan and execute an experiment
* (b) the artificial nature of the laboratory setting interferes with the generalization of the results
(c) inadequacy of the approach as a method of scientific inquiry into the study of human behavior
(d) none of the above

7. In psychological experimentation the term phenomenon refers to:

(a) cause-effect relationships
(b) experimental results
(c) independent variable
* (d) publicly observable behavior
(e) controlled observation

8. Which of the following is a valid criticism of the experimental approach?

* (a) artificiality of the laboratory
(b) the approach is inadequate
(c) the approach promotes the view that humans are manipulable
(d) the approach is not appropriate for studying human behavior

9. Advantages of the experimental approach include:

(a) control of extraneous variables
(b) ability to manipulate one or more variables
(c) suggests new studies
* (d) all of the above

10. All of the following are disadvantages of the experimental approach except:

(a) artificial environments
(b) time consuming
(c) difficult to design
* (d) lack of control

11. The experimental approach is used in:

(a) laboratory settings
(b) field settings
* (c) a and b
(d) none of the above

12. The primary advantage of the experimental approach is:

(a) ability to generalize
(b) lack of artificiality
* (c) control of extraneous variables
(d) suggest solutions to practical problems

13. The advantage of the field experiment is that:

* (a) artificiality is minimized
(b) control over extraneous variables is easier
(c) the results from the field experiment are more conclusive than from other techniques
(d) it is easier to manipulate variables

14. The "rule of one variable" in an experiment is:

(a) only one variable may be studied at a time
* (b) all conditions must be constant except one, which is varied and the results measured
(c) the dimensions of one variable must be known
(d) one condition must be constant and the other conditions varied and measured

15. Which of the following is an example of phenomenon in psychological experimentation?

(a) publicly observable actions
(b) verbal statements
(c) questionnaire responses
(d) physiological recordings
* (e) all of the above are examples of a phenomenon

16. A field experiment is an experimental research study that

(a) is conducted in a laboratory setting to maximize control over extraneous variables
(b) is conducted in an obtrusive manner, with no variables manipulated
* (c) is conducted in a natural setting with as many extraneous variables controlled for as the situation will allow
(d) is conducted via naturalistic observation, with no variables manipulated

17. To study the immediate effect of cocaine on memory, Dr. W. has group A ingest two grams of cocaine, and gives group B two grams of a placebo. This method of determining causation is called

(a) method of concomitant variation
(b) joint method of agreement and differences
(c) method of agreement
* (d) none of the above

18. A researcher notes that cigarette smokers are prone to developing lung cancer, and that this is true regardless of the brand of cigarette smoked. He concludes that the paper used to roll the cigarettes must be the cause of lung cancer. This is the __________ of determining causation.

(a) joint methods of agreement and difference
* (b) method of agreement
(c) method of concomitant variation
(d) none of the above

19. Researcher X wants to know if drinking greater amounts of alcohol is accompanied by a greater difficulty in problem solving. To determine this, she would use the

* (a) method of concomitant variation
(b) method of difference
(c) method of agreement
(d) none of the above

20. Which method provides the most information about how a variable affects the behavior?

(a) method of agreement
(b) method of difference
(c) joint methods of agreement and difference
* (d) method of concomitant variation

21. If a selection bias exists in an experiment then

(a) one cannot make causal statements
* (b) the results may lack in generalizability
(c) it is better to use a correlational approach
(d) a and b

22. For a condition to qualify as a cause of some effect, it must be

(a) necessary
(b) sufficient
(c) observable
* (d) a and b

23. The belief that the best status a theory or prediction can attain is one of "not yet disconfirmed" is referred to as

(a) a necessary condition
* (b) position of falsification
(c) a sufficient condition
(d) position of justification

24. Popper takes a falsification position by stating that the best status a theory can attain is one of:

(a) not yet confirmed
(b) not yet proven
* (c) not yet disconfirmed
(d) none of the above

25. Popper's falsification position states that:

* (a) a theory or prediction can be falsified but never confirmed by research
(b) a theory is false until proven true
(c) a theory is accepted as true until disconfirmed
(d) a theory is not disconfirmed even though studies don't support it

Fill In The Blank

1. The experimental research approach has come to represent the prototype of the scientific method for problem solving because of its ability to identify ______________.
(causation)

2. A _____________ _____________ may by described as an objective observation of phenomena that are made to occur in a strictly controlled situation in which one or more factors are varied and the others are kept constant.
(psychological experiment)

3. The investigator must exhibit _____________, or impartiality and freedom from bias.
(objectivity)

4. B. F. Skinner is an example of those psychologists who believe that psychology should study only _____________ phenomena and ignore anything that cannot be observed or that must be inferred.
(environmental)

5. _____________ refers to the need to eliminate the influence of variables other than those manipulated by the experimenter.
(control)

6. Although there are several advantages of the experimental approach, the first and foremost advantage is that __________ can be exercised.
(control)

7. The idea of __________ refers to controlling or eliminating the influence of all variables except the one or ones of interest.
(constancy)

8. The idea of __________ means that one or more variables must be deliberately and precisely varied by some given amount to determine their effect on behavior.
(variation)

9. The experimental approach is most often used in a _____________ setting.
(laboratory)

10. Researchers using field experiments do not have to worry about the problem of _____________ .
(artificiality)

11. The primary difficulty with field experiments is that control of_____________ cannot be accomplished as well as with laboratory experiments.
(extraneous variables)

12. Identification of causation requires direct _____________ of the variables of interest.
(manipulation)

13. Mill's Method of Concomitant Variation is aimed at identifying the parallel __________ which exists in two variables.
(variation)

14. To state that a cause has been found for an event means that both the _________ and __________ conditions have been found.
(necessary; sufficient)

15. The most frequently cited disadvantage of the experimental approach is that laboratory findings are obtained in an artificial and sterile atmosphere making _____________ to real-life situations difficult.
(generalization)

16. The experimental approach is typically used in two different research settings--a _____________ setting and a _____________ setting.
(laboratory; field)

17. While the _____________ will most likely continue to be the most frequent setting for experimentation, there is a move for an increase in _____________ experimentation.
(laboratory; field)

18. The method by which one identifies causality by observing the common elements that exist in several instances of an event is referred to as the method of _____________
(agreement)

19. The method of ___________ ___________ states that a variable is either a cause or an effect, or else is connected through some factor of causation, if variation in the variable results in a parallel variation in another variable.
(concomitant variation)

20. In the method of __________, one attempts to identify causality by observing the different effects produced in two situations that are alike in all respects except one.
(difference)

21. A __________ condition is one that must be present in order for the effect to occur.
(necessary)

22. A condition that will always produce the effect under study is referred to as a __________ condition.
(sufficient)

23. The belief that the best status a theory or prediction can attain is one of "not yet falsified" is referred to as a __________ __________ .
(position of falsification)

24. When one identifies water as an intoxicant because it is the common element in many intoxicating drinks he is using Mill's method of __________ .
(agreement)

True and False

1. Complete objectivity on the part of the investigator is an absolute necessity in order to be able to identify causation.
(False)

2. The experimental research approach is one that attempts to identify correlational relationships among variables.
(False)

3. The experimental approach to research is the most widely used method.
(False)

4. The experimental approach has become the prototype scientific method for problem solving.
(True)

5. An advantage of the experimental approach is that causal evidence can be obtained.
(True)

6. In a psychological experiment, only one factor may be varied at a time while the others are held constant.
(False)

7. Not all psychologists accept the position that the phenomena under objective observation must be a publicly observable behavior.
(True)

8. In an experiment, the experimenter precisely manipulates one or more variables and objectively observes the phenomena that are made to occur by this manipulation.
(True)

9. One way of achieving control in an experiment is by conducting the experiment in a natural setting, rather than bringing it into the artificial setting of a laboratory.
(False)

10. Use of the experimental approach has produced results that have stood the test of time, suggested areas for future research, and have suggested solutions to practical problems.
(True)

11. Since laboratory experiments are conducted in sterile and well-controlled environments, this makes the findings more generalizable to real-life situations.
(False)

12. In a field experiment conducted in a natural setting, the experimenter actively manipulates variables and carefully controls the influence of as many extraneous variables as the situation will permit.
(True)

13. While the two studies share the same strengths, the laboratory study and the field study differ in terms of their weaknesses.
(False)

14. The experimental approach can be used in a field setting.
(True)

15. If unequivocal results are obtained in the laboratory, they need not be verified before generalizing to the real world.
(False)

16. Even though precise results can be obtained from the laboratory, applicability of these results to the real world must always be verified.
(True)

17. With the method of difference, one attempts to identify causality by observing the different effects produced in two situations that are alike in all respects except one.
(True)

18. John Stuart Mill's canons of causality give psychological researchers a means for experimentally identifying causality.
(False)

19. A necessary condition refers to a condition that will always produce the effect.
(False)

20. A condition that must be present in order for the effect to occur is referred to as a necessary condition.
(True)

21. A sufficient condition is one that will always produce the effect under study.
(True)

22. According to Popper (1968), a theory or prediction can be confirmed or disproven; this is referred to as the position of falsification.
(False)

Chapter 5

Problem Identification and Hypothesis Formation

Multiple Choice:

1. A theory may be described as

   (a) the best prediction or a tentative solution to a problem
   (b) a group of logically organized and inductively related laws
   (c) an interrogative sentence that states the relationship between two variables
 * (d) a group of logically organized and deductively related laws

2. Which of the following is not true of theories?

   (a) summarize and integrate existing knowledge
   (b) guide research
 * (c) a group of logically organized and inductively related laws
   (d) a group of logically organized and deductively related laws

3. Which of the following statements are true?

 * (a) books are generally the outgrowth of work cited in journals
   (b) journal articles are usually the outgrowth of work cited in books
   (c) manually performing a literature review is becoming more practical
   (d) the volumes of Psychology Abstracts have quadrupled in the past ten years

4. Two functions of theory have been characterized as:

 * (a) tool and goal
   (b) goal and hypothesis formation
   (c) causative determination and prediction
   (d) rule and school
   (e) tool and causative determining

5. All of the following are sources of research problems except:

   (a) everyday life
   (b) theories
   (c) previous research
 * (d) proposed future research
   (e) practical issues

6. A psychologist attempts to investigate problems that a particular industry is facing with employee morale, absenteeism and turnover. From which of the following sources did this psychologist obtain this experimental problem?

  (a) theory
* (b) practical issues
  (c) past research
  (d) everyday life

7. Which of the following sources of research ideas is especially good since it is not only designed to provide additional knowledge, but also tends to generate more questions than it answers?

  (a) practical issues
  (b) everyday life
* (c) past research
  (d) theory

8. After a topic of research has been selected, the next step in the research process is to

  (a) formulate a hypothesis
  (b) formulate a research problem
  (c) design the experiment
* (d) review information available on the topic

9. Conducting a thorough review of the literature prior to beginning a research project is important because it will point out

  (a) whether the problem you have identified has already been researched
  (b) if you are knowledgeable enough in the area to conduct the research
  (c) methodological problems specific to the area of study
* (d) a and c

10. An investigator's manuscript was not accepted for publication because many of the same studies had already been conducted. Perhaps the investigator should have spent more time at which step before submitting the article?

  (a) problem identification
  (b) hypothesis formation
* (c) literature review
  (d) designing the experiment
  (e) statistical analysis

11. The *Annual Review of Psychology* represents which type of literature review source?

(a) psychological abstract
(b) information retrieval system
(c) psychological journal
* (d) book
(e) psychological association conference

12. A literature search of material published prior to 1967:

(a) can be conducted by PASAR
* (b) must be conducted by the individual investigator
(c) can be conducted by ERIC
(d) can be conducted by Computer Search Incorporated (CPI)

13. Which of the following is not true of PASAR?

(a) it is an acronym for Psychological Abstracts Search and Retrieval
(b) it is a nonprofit organization operated by APA
* (c) it provides services free of charge
(d) it cannot search material earlier than 1967
(e) it makes use of psychological abstracts

14. The comprehensive information storage and retrieval system operated by the American Psychological Association is referred to as

* (a) PASAR
(b) Psychological Abstracts
(c) *Annual Review of Psychology*
(d) none of the above

15. Which alternative would be the most helpful to know when searching for an article via psychological abstracts?

(a) the author
* (b) the category or topic
(c) the journal in which the article is published
(d) the date of publication
(e) the university from which it was published

16. PASAR makes use of:

(a) books
* (b) the psychological abstracts
(c) ERIC
(d) The *Annual Review of Psychology*
(e) author indexes

17. An excellent source of current information on a particular topic is:

(a) very recent publications
* (b) psychological association conference
(c) Annual Review of Psychology
(d) Current Topics In Psychology

18. Which of the following steps immediately follows the literature review?

(a) designing the study
(b) collection of data
* (c) research problem formulation
(d) operationally defining the variable of interest
(e) hypothesis formation

19. Which of the following is not a criterion which good research problems must meet?

(a) the problem should be stated as a question
* (b) the problem should be an extension of past research
(c) the problem should be empirically testable
(d) the variables expressed in the problem should express a relation

20. Specificity in a research question:

* (a) helps insure that the investigator understands the problem
(b) should depend on amount of past research conducted on the particular topic
(c) theoretically should be independent of the purpose of the problem statement
(d) a and b
(e) all of the above

21. Consider the following research questions:

(1) What are the effects of the environment on learning ability?
(2) What is the effect of word length on memory for a word?

Which statement is true concerning these questions?

* (a) both meet the criteria for good research questions, but #1 lacks specificity
(b) neither meets the criteria for a good research question
(c) both are equally acceptable research questions
(d) statement #1 is more valuable because it allows for more variables to be investigated

22. What should be considered when assessing whether or not your research problem is a good one?

(a) is the problem stated in question form?
(b) does the problem express a relation between the variables?
(c) is it possible to test the problem empirically?
(c) a and b
* (e) all of the above

23. In formulating a problem, the preciseness with which the research question is stated is an important consideration. This is referred to as the

* (a) specificity of the research question
(b) research problem
(c) null hypothesis
(d) none of the above

24. The predicted relationship among the variables being investigated is commonly referred to as the

(a) null hypothesis
(b) research problem
* (c) scientific hypothesis
(d) specificity of the research question

25. To obtain support for the scientific hypothesis, you must collect evidence that will enable you to

* (a) reject the null hypothesis
(b) confirm the research question
(c) accept the null hypothesis
(d) b and c

26. If the hypothesis is not confirmed by the experiment, it means that either the hypothesis is false or some error exists in the conception of the hypothesis. If a conceptual error exists, it may be that

(a) the experimenter misinterpreted some of the literature
(b) some relevant information may have been overlooked in the literature review
(c) the information obtained from prior experiments may be false
(d) b and c
* (e) all of the above

27. Which of the following statements is correct with regard to hypothesis formation?

(a) it represents the best prediction or tentative solution to a problem
(b) it logically follows the statement of the problem
(e) it is often a function of the literature review
(d) it is frequently formulated from theory
* (e) all of the above are correct

28. Which is true concerning hypotheses?

(a) they can at times precede a research question
(b) they must be stated for a study to serve a purpose
* (c) they must be capable of being refuted or confirmed
(d) they need not follow a research question
(e) they are unrelated to past research

29. Which of the following is false?

(a) hypotheses function to support literature that suggested the hypothesis as well as identify a number of errors in the hypothesis or the experimental procedure
(b) information retrieval systems are more costly to use than psychological journals
* (c) a good research problem must have empirical support: that is, it must be based upon past research
(d) hypotheses clearly state a problem
(e) direct communication is a very good literature review technique to acquire current information

30. Which of the following statements is false?

(a) in any study it is the null hypothesis that is always tested
* (b) in any study it is the scientific hypothesis that is always tested
(c) the null hypothesis represents a statement of no relationship between the variables under study
(d) support for the scientific hypothesis is always obtained indirectly by rejecting the null hypothesis

31. What is the most important issue to consider when formulating the research question?

(a) it should be based on theory
(b) it should be based on conclusions from prior research
(c) it should be comprehensive
* (d) it should be very specific
(e) it should be general

32. *The Thesaurus of Psychological Index Terms:*

(a) identifies terms that relate to the topic
(b) defines psychological terms
(c) identifies the appropriate journals to use
(d) is an appropriate beginning point in a literature review
* (e) all of the above

33. Where does one look for a good problem to research?

(a) questions of everyday life
(b) practical issues which need solutions
(c) theories
(d) research done by others
* (e) all of the above

34. The two primary sources of information about a research topic are:

(a) books and your professor
* (b) books and journals
(c) journals and nationwide conventions
(d) national and regional conventions

35. When formulating a research question a rule of thumb to follow is:

* (a) be specific
(b) be comprehensive
(c) be general
(d) both a and b

36. The one criteria which a scientific hypothesis must meet is that it must be:

(a) specific
* (b) capable of being refuted
(c) concisely stated in question form

Fill In The Blank

1. Typical sources psychologists may use for research problems include practical issues, everyday events, _____________, and _____________.
(theory, past research)

2. A_____________ is defined as a group of logically organized and deductively related laws.
(theory)

3. The ____________ function of theory is evidenced by the idea that theories summarize and integrate existing knowledge.
(goal)

4. The _____________ function of theory is evidenced by the proposition that theories guide research.
(tool)

5. Theory has both a ____________ and a ______________ function.
(tool, goal)

6. The first step in conducting a research study is ____________ _____________ .
(literature review)

7. A _____________ is a group of logically organized and deductively related laws.
(theory)

8. Books, psychological journals, and information retrieval systems are all examples of sources available for conducting __________ ___________ .
(literature reviews)

9. __________ __________is a journal that contains abstracts of books, journal and technical reports, monographs, and other scientific documents.
(Psychological Abstracts)

10. A __________ ___________ asks what relationship exists between two or more variables.
(research problem)

11. After completing the literature review, one formulates a___________ ___________, an interrogative sentence that states the relationship between two variables.
(research problem)

12. ____________ is a comprehensive information storage and retrieval system.
(PASAR)

13. The rule of thumb in formulating a research question is be ______________.
(specific)

14. ____________ represent predictions or tentative solutions to the problem being researched.
(Hypotheses)

15. After the literature review has been completed and the problem has been stated in question form, the next step is to begin formulating the ____________ .
(hypothesis)

16. __________ __________ contain brief summaries of published journal articles.
(Psychological Abstracts)

17. A hypothesis must be capable of being ____________ or __________.
(refuted; confirmed)

18. The primary criterion which a hypothesis must meet is that of ___________.
(testability)

19. The ___________ __________ states that no difference will be found between the variables being investigated.
(null hypothesis)

20. The __________ hypothesis is always tested in a research study.
(null)

21. While the __________ hypothesis represents the predicted relationship among the variables being investigated, the __________ hypothesis represents a statement of no relationship among the variables being investigated.
(scientific, null)

22. In any study, it is the ____________ hypothesis that is always tested, because the __________ hypothesis does not specify the exact amount or type of influence that is expected.
(null, scientific)

23. To obtain support for the scientific hypothesis, evidence must be collected that allows the ____________ of the null hypothesis.
(rejection)

<u>True and False</u>

1. Hypotheses are a source of research problems.
(False)

2. An excellent source of information on a particular topic is very recent publications.
(False)

3. Typical sources for research problems in psychology include theory, everyday events, past research, and practical issues.
(True)

4. A theory, as defined by Marx (1963), is a group of logically organized and inductively related laws.
(False)

5. Previously conducted experiments are an excellent source of research ideas since research tends to generate more questions than it asks.
(True)

6. After selecting a topic for research, the next step is to formulate the hypothesis.
(False)

7. Formulation of the research problem logically follows the literature review.
(True)

8. A theory is a group of logically organized and deductively related laws.
(True)

9. A literature review is necessary only when one intends to publish a study.
(False)

10. The general purpose of the literature review is to gain an understanding of the current state of knowledge about the topic.
(True)

11. The *Annual Review of Psychology* is a journal that contains abstracts of books, journal and technical reports, monographs, and other scientific documents.
(False)

12. Due to the drastic increase in the amount of published information available, manually performed comprehensive literature searches are becoming less practical and are being replaced by information storage and retrieval systems such as **PASAR.**
(True)

13. *Psychological Abstracts* is a comprehensive information storage and retrieval system operated by the American Psychological Association.
(False)

14. The primary purposes of formulating the research problem in question form are to ensure that the researcher has a good grasp of the variables to be investigated and to aid the experimenter in conducting the literature review.
(False)

15. The hypothesis is the best prediction or a tentative solution to a problem.
(True)

16. In an experimental study it is the scientific hypothesis that is being tested.
(False)

17. To obtain support for the scientific hypothesis, evidence must be collected that enables the experimenter to accept the null hypothesis.
(False)

18. In most studies it is the scientific hypothesis that is tested.
(False)

19. The scientific hypothesis must be true if the null hypothesis is rejected.
(False)

20. A research problem is an interrogative statement which states the relationship which exists between two variables
(True)

21. Previously conducted research is an excellent source of research ideas.
(True)

Chapter 6

Variables Used in Experimentation

Multiple Choice:

1. In any given study, there are many possible independent and dependent variables that could be used. The variables to be used are specified by the

* (a) research problem
(b) hypothesis
(c) literature review
(d) b and c

2. An antecedent condition manipulated by the experimenter is referred to as the

(a) behavioral effect
(b) dependent variable
(c) event manipulation
* (d) independent variable

3. The variable which is manipulated by the experimenter is the

* (a) independent variable
(b) dependent variable
(c) control variable
(d) correlated variable

4. Which of the following is false with regard to the independent variable?

(a) it represents the antecedent conditions manipulated by the experimenter
(b) it is varied through a defined range
* (c) it measures the influence of the manipulation
(d) it is the variable whose effect is being tested
(e) a study can have several independent variables

5. The dependent variable:

* (a) measures the influence of experimental manipulation
(b) determines the amount of manipulation to be used
(c) is independent of the independent variable
(d) is the variable whose effect is being tested
(e) must be influenced by many other factors than the independent variable

6. In a study investigating the influence of aggressive behavior on emotionality, aggression would be the:

   (a) dependent variable
* (b) independent variable
   (c) either the dependent or independent variable
   (d) none of the above

7. For a variable to qualify as an independent variable, it must:

   (a) be manipulated
   (b) have variation
   (c) have controlled variation
   (d) be under direct control of the experimenter
* (e) all of the above

8. There are several techniques for achieving variation in the independent variable. Which of the following is <u>not</u> one of these techniques?

   (a) presence versus absence
   (b) type of a variable
* (c) level of a variable
   (d) amount of a variable

9. The presence versus absence technique is:

   (a) a way to eliminate or minimize variation
   (b) a technique where one group receives treatment while the other group is absent
   (c) a situation where two or more groups receive treatments in the absence of the experimenter
* (d) a situation where one group receives a treatment and the other group does not
   (e) a and d

10. In a drug study variation would be achieved by:

   (a) "presence versus absence" technique
   (b) "amount of variable" technique
   (c) "type of variable" technique
* (d) any of the above depending on the research problem

11. A technique for achieving variation in the independent variable involves:

   (a) varying the number of subjects receiving the treatment
* (b) varying the amount of the variable that subjects receive
   (c) holding the dependent variable constant
   (d) none of the above

12. In order to test the hypothesis, abstract conceptual variables must be translated into

* (a) concrete experimental operations
(b) concepts
(c) a standard agreed upon technique
(d) a dependent variable

13. How many levels of variation should be produced by the independent variable?

(a) as many as possible
(b) at least four
(c) no more than four
* (d) at least two
(e) only one if possible

14. One way to achieve variation in the independent variable is to:

(a) vary the number of dependent variables
(b) vary the type of dependent variable
(c) vary the experimenters manipulating the variables
(d) all of the above
* (e) none of the above

15. Which of the following may be used to establish variation in the independent variable?

(a) instructional manipulation
(b) event manipulation
(c) setting manipulation
* (d) a and b
(e) b and c

16. Experimental manipulation refers to:

(a) random manipulation of the dependent variable
* (b) controlled manipulation of the independent variable
(c) random manipulation of the independent variable
(d) controlled manipulation of the dependent variable
(e) none of the above

17. Two basic ways an experimenter can experimentally manipulate the independent variable are:

(a) manipulation of instructions and subject assignment
* (b) manipulation of events and instructions
(c) manipulation of subject category and amount of the independent variable
(d) manipulation of events and subject assignment
(e) manipulation of instructions and subject category

18. Risks involved in instructional manipulation include:

(a) individual differences in the interpretations of the instructions
(b) misinterpretations of instructions
(c) subject inattentiveness
* (d) all of the above
(e) none of the above

19. Problems with subjects being inattentive and subject-to-subject variation are dangers associated with which type of independent variable manipulation?

* (a) instructional manipulation
(b) measured manipulation
(c) event manipulation
(d) all of the above

20. Disadvantage(s) of manipulation of variables through instruction is (are)

(a) misinterpretations of instructions
(b) subject inattentiveness
(c) no more than one variable can be effectively manipulated
* (d) all of the above

21. If given a choice between manipulation of events or manipulation of instruction the best choice is usually

* (a) events
(b) instructions
(c) a combination of both

22. In a drug study which of the following could be the independent variable?

(a) drug dosage
(b) drug type
(c) effect of the drug on high vs. low anxiety subjects
(d) drug induced by pill vs. injection
* (e) all of the above

23. The assumption underlying which technique of manipulating the independent variable is based on the premise that individuals possess a certain amount of a variety of variables, commonly labeled personality variables?

(a) event manipulation
* (b) individual difference manipulation
(c) instructional manipulation
(d) none of the above

24. Which of the following techniques for achieving construct validity does not fall under the heading of manipulation checks?

(a) interview subject after the independent variable has been introduced to determine whether the desired construct was actually attained
* (b) provide a clear definition of the abstract construct
(c) get a behavioral indicator that the experimental operations are arousing the desired effect
(d) pretesting

25. Construct validity refers to the extent to which the higher order construct:

(a) correlates with theoretical definitions of that construct
* (b) can be inferred from the empirical operations used to represent the construct
(c) correlates with definitions of the construct agreed upon by researchers in the field
(d) correlates with the less abstract lower order construct

26. Evidence for construct validity can be obtained by collecting:

(a) predictive data
(b) convergent data
(c) divergent data
* (d) b and c
(e) none of the above

27. As meaningfulness of manipulation of events in social research increases, __________ decreases.

(a) impact
* (b) control
(c) importance
(d) relevance

28. Which of the following is not a way to provide assurance of construct validity when using human subjects?

(a) conduct interviews with the subject after the independent variable has been introduced
(b) get a behavioral indicator that signifies the manipulations are arousing the desired effect
(c) pretesting to get an indication of the level of intensity
* (d) none of the above

29. It is the task of the dependent variable to

(a) determine whether or not the independent variable produced an effect
(b) indicate if the effect was facilitating or inhibiting
(c) reveal the magnitude of the effect
* (d) all the above
(e) a and b only

30. Which of the following is true with regard to a dependent variable?

(a) it determines whether the independent variable produced an effect
(b) it determines whether an effect was facilitative
(c) it determines whether an effect was inhibitory
(d) it can reveal magnitude of the effect
* (e) all of the above

31. The response that should be selected as the dependent variable is:

(a) an internal state
(b) an overt response
* (c) the response most sensitive to the independent variable
(d) a physiological response

32. If organisms consistently respond in the same way to the dependent variable, then it is:

(a) valid
* (b) reliable
(c) valid and reliable
(d) unreliable but invalid
(e) unreliable and invalid

33. The extent to which the same results are obtained when responses are measured at different times is referred to as

* (a) reliability
(b) validity
(c) independent manipulation
(d) subject error

34. Which of the following statements are true?

- (a) validity is usually easier to obtain than reliability
- * (b) reliability is usually easier to obtain than validity
- (c) experimenters often concern themselves with validity
- (d) validity is of minor importance when compared to reliability
- (e) a concise operational definition is a good substitute for construct validity

35. If a change in "A" will result in a change in "Z" then "Z" is

- (a) an independent variable
- (b) a reliable variable
- (c) a valid variable
- * (d) a dependent variable

36. Which of the following is not a technique for disguising the dependent variable?

- (a) assess the dependent variable in a setting different from the experiment
- * (b) assess behavior that is not significant to the subject
- (c) construct a study so that the subject doesn't know that the dependent variable is being observed
- (d) disguise the reason for interest in a particular dependent variable
- (e) imbed key items in a larger questionnaire

37. When more than one dependent variable can be used, the scientist:

- * (a) typically selects one
- (b) will use at least two dependent variables
- (c) will select as many as can be handled effectively
- (d) always uses more than one dependent variable

38. Conducting an obtrusive experiment is one means of:

- * (a) reducing subject error
- (b) attaining reliability
- (c) attaining validity
- (d) assuring that the concrete operations represent the conceptual variable

39. In order for an independent variable to be used in an experiment it must:

(a) be reliable
* (b) be translated into concrete experimental operations
(c) be valid
(d) be presented in at least one form
(e) be controlled

40. Which of the following is a method to reduce subject error?

(a) assess the dependent variable outside the experimental setting
(b) assess behavior of significance to the subject
(c) use confederates to assess the dependent variable
(d) use unsuspicious subjects
* (e) all of the above

41. If I make reference to some characteristic of an organism, environment or experiment situation I am referring to a:

(a) manipulation
* (b) variable
(c) specific event
(d) higher order construct
(e) construct validity

42. The extent to which the experimenter is measuring what he/she wants to measure is referred to as

(a) reliability
(b) subject error
* (c) validity
(d) operational definition

43. An experimenter is trying to assure construct validity in a study on depression. The results show that the measure of depression this experimenter is using is highly correlated with other measures claiming to be indices of depression. This indicates that the experimenter has obtained

(a) reliable data
* (b) convergent data
(c) divergent data
(d) unreliable data

44. An experimenter wants to reduce subject error when assessing the dependent variable in his study. What procedure can he use?

(a) disguise the reason for interest in a particular dependent variable
(b) have a confederate collect the data
(c) assess the dependent variable outside the context of the experiment
* (d) all of the above
(e) none of the above

Fill In The Blank

1. An experimenter manipulates drug dosage to observe the effects of the drug on the amount of sleep subjects get at night. The __________ variable is drug dose.
(independent)

2. Three ways to vary an independent variable are to vary: __________, __________ , and __________ .
(presence vs. absence, amount, type)

3. The ________variable refers to the measurement of the effect of the __________ variable.
(dependent; independent)

4. The__________ __________ is the response of the organism, or the variable that measures the influence of the independent variable.
(dependent variable)

5. A __________ is any characteristic or phenomenon that can vary across organisms, situations, or environments.
(variable)

6. In the _________ _________ __________ technique for achieving variation in the independent variable, one group of subjects receives the treatment condition and the other group does not.
(presence versus absence)

7. There must be at least _________ levels of variation and the levels must always differ from each other.
(two)

8. The term __________ __________ refers to a situation in which the experimenter administers one specific controlled amount of a variable to one group of individuals and a different specific controlled amount of the same variable to a second group of individuals.
(experimental manipulation)

9. An experimenter varying the independent variable by giving different sets of instructions to the subjects is using the technique of __________.
(instructional manipulation)

10. When one varies the independent variable by altering the events that subjects experience, one is using the __________ __________ technique.
(event manipulation)

11. The term __________ __________ __________ refers to the situation in which the independent variable is varied by selecting subjects that differ in terms of some measured internal state.
(individual difference manipulation)

12. If a measure of a construct consistently yields the same results this means that the measure is __________.
(reliable)

13. If the dependent variable is __________, then it will measure what you want it to measure.
(valid)

14. Probably no more than __________ variable(s) should be manipulated through instructions.
(one)

15. When a choice exists between using instructions or events to create variation, the best choice is usually __________.
(events)

16. Typically, as control over variables is increased, the impact of the experiment is __________.
(decreased)

17. Individual difference manipulations refer to varying the independent variable by measuring different amounts or types of an __________ state.
(internal)

18. The more commitment demanded of the subject by the dependent variable, the __________ the degree of confidence one can have in the results of an experiment.
(greater)

19. The reliability of dependent variable responses increases as the number of response measures __________.
(increase)

20. Difficulty in translating the independent variable into concrete operational terms arises when the independent variable consists of some _________ __________ such as anxiety, frustration, or attitude.
(abstract construct)

21. The differential effect that one independent variable has for each level of one or more additional independent variables is referred to as the _________.
(interaction)

22. Variation in the independent variable can be created by varying the __________ or __________ of the independent variable.
(type; amount)

23. The dependent variable is the one designed to measure the effect of variation of the __________.
(independent variable)

24. Evidence for construct validity can be obtained by collecting convergent and __________ data.
(divergent)

25. In single-occasion events, the subject comes to the experiment one time and the dependent variable is only measured once. Consequently, the __________ of the dependent variable cannot be assessed.
(reliability)

26. An experimenter disguises the reason for interest in a particular dependent variable and uses a physiological measure that is presumably not under the subject's control; the experimenter is interested in reducing _________ __________ when assessing the dependent variable.
(subject error)

<u>True and False</u>

1. A variable is any characteristic or phenomenon that can vary across organisms, situations, or environments.
(True)

2. The independent variable is the response of the organism.
(False)

3. If you were studying the effectiveness of several treatments for depression, the task of the dependent variable would be to assess the effectiveness of these treatments.
(True)

4. One of the antecedent conditions manipulated by the experimenter is referred to as the independent variable.
(True)

5. The dependent variable is defined as the antecedent conditions which are manipulated by the experimenter.
(False)

6. In a properly controlled experiment, the value of the dependent variable is held constant.
(False)

7. Varying the drug dosage is an example of independent variable manipulation by manipulation of events.
(True)

8. In using interviews as checks on the validity of operational definitions, it is important that the interviews follow immediately after the administration of the treatment conditions.
(True)

9. It is the task of the independent variable to determine the effects of the dependent variable.
(False)

10. The term instructional manipulation refers to the situation in which the independent variable is varied by selecting subjects that differ in the amount or type of a measured internal state.
(False)

11. Event manipulation varies the independent variable by altering the events that subjects experience.
(True)

12. When one has difficulty in translating the dependent variable into concrete operational terms, it is based on the fact that there is no one single definition or empirical referent.
(False)

13. One manipulation check that can be used to provide assurance of construct validity involves getting a behavioral indicator that the experimental operations are arousing the desired effect.
(True)

14. One manipulation check that can be used to provide assurance of construct validity involves conducting interviews with the subject after the dependent variable has been introduced to determine whether the desired construct was actually attained.
(False)

15. When deciding on how many independent variables to include, one should keep in mind that behavior is multidetermined, and inclusion of more than one independent variable is often desirable because of the added information it will give in the form of an interaction.
(True)

16. It is the function of the dependent variable to determine whether or not the independent variable produced an effect, whether the effect was facilitating or inhibiting, and to reveal the magnitude of the effect.
(True)

17. Establishing the validity of the dependent variable is in most cases more difficult than establishing its reliability.
(True)

18. There are specific rules to follow that will pinpoint the most appropriate dependent variable to use.
(False)

19. Establishing the validity of the dependent variable involves obtaining evidence that the dependent variable actually measures the construct we want it to measure.
(True)

20. It is not always necessary to specify the exact empirical operations that define the independent variable.
(False)

21. In animal research the problem of realistic situations seldom exists.
(True)

22. In research involving social interaction, as realism of social experiences increases, control is usually increased.
(False)

23. One way to establish variation in the independent variable is through manipulation of events.
(True)

24. Varying the type of variable is an appropriate way to achieve variation in the dependent variable.
(False)

25. Manipulation of instructions is the best technique for varying independent variables.
(False)

26. If a measure of a construct consistently yields the same results this indicates that the measure is reliable.
(True)

27. Theoretically the number of independent variables that can be varied should be limited to three.
(False)

28. Divergent data are data that indicated that the dependent variable is measuring the same thing as are other measures of the same construct.
(False)

29. Disguising the reason for interest in a particular dependent variable, assessing the dependent variable outside the context of the experiment, and having a confederate collect the data are but several procedures that can be used to reduce experimenter error when assessing the dependent variable.
(False)

30. If the results of an experiment are reliable then they are necessarily valid.
(False)

Chapter 7

Control in Experimentation

<u>Multiple Choice</u>

1. In most cases it is possible to:

   (a) eliminate the effects of extraneous variables
   * (b) eliminate the differential effects of extraneous variables
   (c) keep all factors constant throughout the experiment
   (d) select subjects having an identical amount of particular characteristics

2. An experimenter wants to be sure the observed effect is caused only by the experimental treatment condition. He wants to achieve

   (a) construct validity
   * (b) internal validity
   (c) face validity
   (d) reliability

3. An extraneous variable is

   * (a) any variable other than the independent variable that influences the dependent variable
   (b) any variable under the experimenter's control
   (c) any variable that measures the influence of the independent variable
   (d) any variable that measures the magnitude of the dependent variable

4. Although it may not be possible to eliminate all extraneous variables it is possible to hold many of them constant across various levels of the independent variable. However, there are some variables that cannot be held completely constant because

   (a) they are difficult to operationally define
   (b) constancy requires an exact measure which may not be possible due the nature of the variable and our measuring devices
   (c) some variables present in an experiment may change as the experiment progresses
   * (d) b and c
   (e) a and c

5. History is an extraneous variable that refers to:

    (a) events that occur before the first measurement of the dependent variable
* (b) events other than the independent variable that occur between the first and second measurement of the dependent variable
    (c) events that occur after the last measurement of the dependent variable
    (d) psychological conditions that change with the passage of time
    (e) changes in the assessment of the dependent variable

6. Which variable represents a specific event that occurs between the first and second measurement of the dependent variable, therefore having possible influence on the postmeasurement?

    (a) instrumentation
    (b) maturation
* (c) history
    (d) mortality

7. In a study, an intelligence test is administered as a dependent measure. Through the course of the study, the experimenter gains mastery and improves her testing administration ability. Therefore, the data collected toward the end of the study is more reliable and valid. This is an example of

    (a) maturation
* (b) instrumentation
    (c) statistical regression
    (d) selection

8. Which of the following is an example of a maturation extraneous variable:

    (a) drowsiness
    (b) age
    (c) fatigue
    (d) hunger
* (e) all of the above

9. Instrumentation refers to:

* (a) changes that occur over time in the measurement of the dependent variable
  (b) changes that occur over time in the procedure that is used
  (c) changes that can be attributed to invalid instruments
  (d) changes that occur as a result of differential selection of subjects
  (e) none of the above

10. Selection bias occurs when:

  (a) subjects for various treatment groups are selected according to the same criteria
  (b) nonrandom subject selection to treatments groups exists
  (c) subjects for various treatment groups are selected according to different criteria
  (d) subjects are randomly assigned to treatment groups
* (e) b and c

11. The selection effect is most commonly due to:

* (a) history
  (b) statistical regression
  (c) mortality
  (d) selection
  (e) maturation

12. An intertreatment interaction exists when:

* (a) the motive for positive self-presentation suggests different ways of responding in the various treatment groups
  (b) subjects perceptions of the different treatment condition suggest similar ways of presenting oneself in a positive manner
  (c) subjects perceptions of a treatment condition suggest different ways of presenting oneself in a positive manner
  (d) subjects in the same treatment condition perceive that they can fulfill the positive self-presentation motive by responding in different ways

13. The phenomenon of statistical regression is best described as

* (a) extreme scores in a distribution tending to move toward the mean as a function of repeated testing
(b) changes in the assessment of the dependent variable
(c) an extraneous variable occurring between the pre- and postmeasurement of the dependent variable
(d) a differential loss of subjects from the various experimental groups

14. Extraneous variables can also interact with each other. For example, if a history effect influenced one of two treatment groups, a difference may exist between the two groups not because of the treatment effect but because of the impact of history on only one of the groups. What other variable might history be interacting with in this example to cause only one group to show an effect?

(a) mortality
(b) statistical regression
* (c) selection bias
(d) instrumentation

15. A subject effect is any change in performance that can be attributed to a subject's motives or attitude. Which of the following is not related to this effect?

(a) positive self-presentation
(b) demand characteristics
(c) intratreatment interaction
* (d) maturation

16. The perception by subjects in different treatment groups that they can fulfill the positive self-presentation motive by responding in different ways is referred to as

* (a) intertreatment interaction
(b) demand characteristics
(c) intratreatment interaction
(d) none of the above

17. Which seems to represent the all-encompassing subject motive?

(a) the good subject
(b) the negative subject
(c) evaluation apprehension
* (d) positive self-presentation
(e) the faithful subject

18. Rosenthal (1966) proposed three categories of experimenter attributes which may interact with the independent variable to cause differential performance in subjects. This categorization includes all but which of the following?

(a) biosocial attributes
* (b) physical attributes
(c) psychosocial attributes
(d) situational factors

19. Which of the following is a biosocial attribute of an experimenter?

(a) age
(b) sex
(c) religion
(d) race
* (e) all of the above are biosocial attributes

20. Authoritarianism of the experimenter would be considered as a:

(a) biosocial attribute
* (b) psychosocial attribute
(c) situational factor
(d) biological attribute
(e) sociological attribute

21. One of the few experimenter attributes that has been investigated in depth is:

* (a) sex
(b) race
(c) religion
(d) hostility
(e) authoritarianism

22. Methodologically-sound research must be conducted before anything definitive can be stated about the influence of experimenter attributes on specific types of research. Specifically, there are deficiencies identified by Johnson (1976) that must be overcome. These include

(a) controlling for the confounding influence of attributes other than the ones being studied
(b) taking into account and studying the interactive influence of subject and experimenter attributes
(c) having the researcher sample a variety of types of tasks since an attribute may have an influence on one task but not on another
(d) b and c
* (e) all of the above

23. If subjects are randomly selected and assigned to groups, which extraneous variable cannot be operating?

(a) history effect
(b) apparatus breakdown
(c) experimenter expectancies
(d) mortality
* (e) subject sophistication

24. Future research on experimenter attributes must overcome three deficiencies.
Which of the following is <u>not</u> a deficiency?

(a) the influence of attributes other than the ones being studied
(b) the interactive influence of subject and experimenter attributes
* (c) the influence of subject's motivation
(d) an inadequate variety of types of tasks

25. Which extraneous source of variation can result from subject mortality?

(a) history
* (b) selection
(c) experimenter bias
(d) instrumentation
(e) apparatus breakdown

26. When does the sequencing effect occur?

(a) when subjects have not been randomly assigned to the various conditions
* (b) when participation in one condition affects the response that the subject will make in a subsequent treatment condition
(c) when experimenter expectancy effects have not been controlled for
(d) when the experimenter has not controlled for subject sophistication

27. Which of the following is <u>not</u> true of extraneous variables in psychological research?

(a) some extraneous variables may be kept constant across levels of the independent variable
* (b) it is possible to eliminate the influence of all extraneous variables
(c) ideal constancy can usually be obtained for such variables as sex or rate of presentation but not for factors such as interest
(d) the number and/or type of extraneous variables may change as an experiment proceeds

28. Generally speaking, recording errors in observations:

* (a) infrequently affect the conclusions reached in a study
(b) frequently affect the conclusions reached in a study
(c) are not an important methodological issue
(d) never occur

29. Which of the following is true concerning experimenter expectancy?

* (a) it is not well understood as to how these effects are mediated
(b) expectancy effects probably operate in a unitary fashion
(c) it exists only in human research
(d) it can usually be predicted as to when expectancy effects will occur

30. A possible rival hypothesis in designs with pre and post measurements refers to the fact that extreme scores will tend to move toward the mean of the distribution with repeated testing. This is the __________ effect.

(a) history
(b) selection
(c) maturation
* (d) statistical regression
(e) mortality

31. What might be a potential confound in having subjects respond in all treatment conditions?

(a) mortality
(b) subject bias
(c) selection effect
* (d) sequencing effect
(e) history effect

32. An intratreatment interaction exists when:

(a) subjects in different treatment conditions perceive that they can fulfill the positive self-presentation motive by responding in similar ways
* (b) subjects in the same treatment condition perceive that they can fulfill the positive self-presentation motive by responding in different ways
(c) subjects perceptions of the different treatment conditions suggest similar ways of presenting oneself in a positive manner
(d) the motive for positive self-presentation suggests different ways of responding in the various treatment groups

33. Experimenter expectancy effects are mediated primarily by:

(a) female experimenters
(b) male experimenters
(c) the way the instructions are written
* (d) paralinguistic cues

34. The question as to whether the experimenter is naive or experienced falls under which category?

(a) psychological attributes
* (b) situational factors
(c) biosocial attributes
(d) biopsychological attributes
(e) psychological attributes

35. Debates or controversies in the psychological literature most often center on:

(a) the validity of the data
(b) the accuracy of the observations
(c) the methodology of data collection
* (d) the interpretation of the data
(e) the data recording errors

36. Which of the following would be considered an experimenter attribute?

(a) dominance
(b) need for social approval
(c) intelligence
(d) hostility
* (e) all of the above

37. In a study where subjects received a placebo treatment after a drug treatment, what effect would need to be controlled for?

(a) history effect
(b) statistical regression
(c) selection
(d) experimenter effects
* (e) sequencing

38. When an observed effect is due to the experimental treatment we have:

(a) an ex post facto design
(b) internal analysis
(c) experimental bias
* (d) internal validity
(e) instrumentation

39. Using exactly the same equipment for testing, one set of Firestone tires are road tested in January, and another set are tested in August. It is shown that the tires tested in August wear better. Some conclude that this difference is due to a lack of quality control. What is an alterative explanation?

(a) maturation effect
(b) statistical regression
* (c) history effect
(d) sequencing effect
(e) selection effect

40. A student scores in the extremely bright range on an achievement test. Which of the following points to the fact that this same student probably will not do as well on a second testing?

(a) history
* (b) statistical regression
(c) mortality
(d) selection
(e) maturation

Fill In The Blank

1. Without __________ it would be impossible to identify causation.
(control)

2. An experiment has __________ __________ if the effects obtained in the experiment are due only to the experimental conditions manipulated by the researcher and not to any other variables.
(internal validity)

3. Once an __________ __________ creeps into an experiment, one can no longer draw any conclusion regarding the causal relationship that exists between the independent and the dependent variable.
(extraneous variable)

4. __________ is the stability, or absence of change, in the influence exerted by an extraneous variable in all treatment conditions.
(constancy)

5. In experimentation the desired condition that the scientist strives for is __________ of all variables except the independent variable.
(constancy)

6. Since most variables cannot be eliminated from influencing the experiment, their effect is controlled by holding their effect __________ .
(constant)

7. The __________ variable is an extraneous variable that occurs between the first and second measurement of the dependent variable and therefore could have influenced the postmeasurement.
(history)

8. The variable that refers not to changes in the subject, but to changes that occur in the process of assessment of the dependent variable is referred to as ________________.
(instrumentation)

9. The phenomenon of __________ ___________ is represented by the lowering of extremely high scores and the raising of extremely low scores during posttesting.
(statistical regression)

10. The __________ bias exists when the choice of subjects for the various treatment groups is based on different criteria.
(selection)

11. A __________ bias exists when a different procedure is used for placing subjects in the various comparison groups.
(selection)

12. If a history effect operates along with the independent variable to influence the outcome of a study, the experiment is said to lack internal __________.
(validity)

13. __________ __________ refers to the movement of extreme scores toward the mean of the distribution upon retesting.
(statistical regression)

14. The error of observational attitude is an example of __________ ___________.
(subject bias)

15. __________ __________ are cues in the experiment which indicate to the subject how to respond.
(demand characteristics)

16. Any of the cues available in the experiment, such as the instructions, the experimenter, rumors, or the experimental setting that define the experiment from the subjects' point of view are called __________ __________.
(demand characteristics)

17. __________ refers to the physical and psychological characteristics of experimenters which may create differential responses in subjects.
(experimenter attributes)

18. The story of Clever Hans is an example of __________ __________.
(experimenter bias)

19. Situational factors and psychosocial attributes are two examples of __________.
(experimenter attributes)

20. __________ __________ refers to subject's gain in knowledge about psychology.
(subject sophistication)

21. An __________ interaction exists when different subjects in the same treatment condition perceive different ways of presenting themselves in the most positive light.
(intratreatment)

22. __________ __________ is the biasing influence that can arise from a subject's knowledge of or familiarity with psychology and psychological experiments.
(subject sophistication)

23. The disadvantage to having subjects respond in more than one treatment conditions is that a __________ effect may exist.
(sequencing)

24. Any time a subject's response in one treatment condition is partially determined by participation in a prior treatment condition, __________ effects may occur.
(sequencing)

25. Biosocial attributes are a type of__________ effect.
(experimenter)

True and False

1. The influence of most extraneous variables that could influence a psychological experiment can be eliminated from the experiment.
(False)

2. To the extent that we can accurately state that only the independent variable produced the observed effect can we say that we have achieved internal validity.
(True)

3. An extraneous variable is any variable other than the dependent variable that influences the independent variable.
(False)

4. Generally, the longer the time lapse between the first and second measurement, the greater the possibility of history becoming a rival explanation for the observed effects.
(True)

5. The longer the time lapse between the pre and the posttest, the less the possibility of history becoming a rival explanation.
(False)

6. External validity is attained when the observed effect is due to the experimental treatments.
(False)

7. History refers to the differences in subjects as a result of experiences prior to the experiment.
(False)

8. Maturation refers to the differences occurring within subjects as a result of experiences obtained between pretest and posttest measures of the experiment.
(True)

9. The maturation variable refers to the changes in the external as well as internal conditions of the individual that occur as a function of the passage of time which affect the individual's response to the experimental condition.
(False)

10. In order to eliminate instrumentation effects, studies that use human observers to measure the behavioral characteristics of interest use only one observer so that there will be no differences in the way the data is collected.
(False)

11. The statistical regression phenomenon exists because the first and second measurements of the dependent variable are not perfectly correlated, ie, there is some degree of unreliability in the measuring device.
(True)

12. Mortality refers to the differential loss of subjects from the various experimental groups.
(True)

13. Mortality is not of great concern to researchers who use human subjects because human subjects rarely die during the course of experiment.
(False)

14. When subjects are not randomly chosen and assigned, the existence of a selection bias makes the introduction of rival hypotheses a possibility.
(True)

15. A subject's motivation to respond in such a way as to present themselves in the most positive manner is referred to as a demand characteristic.
(False)

16. An intertreatment interaction exists when different subjects in the same treatment condition perceive different ways of presenting themselves in the most positive light.
(False)

17. The ways in which the experimenter can potentially bias the results of an experiment can be dichotomized into two types: bias arising from the experimenter's attributes and bias resulting from the expectancies of the experimenter.
(True)

18. Experimenter expectancies can operate in a study by having an effect on the subjects, but not on the experimenter himself/herself.
(False)

19. The biasing effects of experimenter expectancies is limited to human types of experimentation.
(False)

20. Maturation effects refer to differential changes of the internal conditions of subjects.
(True)

21. History refers to a source of bias as a result of the subjects experiences prior to the study.
(False)

22. One disadvantage to having subjects participate in all treatment conditions is a possible history effect.
(False)

23. Positive self presentation appears to be the most important subject motive.
(True)

24. When an observed effect can be attributed to the experimental manipulation, the experiment is said to be externally valid.
(False)

25. Carry-over effects may be the result of such factors as practice received or fatigue incurred.
(True)

Chapter 8

Techniques for Achieving Constancy

Multiple Choice

1. Of all the control methods, which is the most important and basic and has the purpose of providing assurance that extraneous variables will not systematically bias the results of the study?

   (a) matching
   * (b) randomization
   (c) counterbalancing
   (d) precision control

2. Randomization:

   (a) always results in an equal distribution of the extraneous variables to be controlled
   (b) is just as effective as any other control technique for controlling unknown extraneous variables
   * (c) implies an assumption of the equiprobability of events
   (d) by itself is sufficient guard for internal validity

3. Concerning randomization, which of the following is false?

   (a) it is the most important of all control methods
   (b) it controls for unknown sources of variation
   (c) it equates groups of subjects
   (d) it controls for known sources of variation
   * (e) it controls for the influence of subject and experimenter effects

4. There are several extraneous variables that are not controlled for by randomization. These include

   * (a) the subject effect and the experimenter effect
   (b) the experimenter effect and statistical regression
   (c) history and mortality
   (d) the subject effect and statistical regression

5. The benefits of using the matching technique include

   (a) decreasing the sensitivity of the experiment
   * (b) the variables on which subjects are matched are controlled in the sense that constancy of influence is attained
   (c) eliminating the need for randomization
   (d) b and c

6. Increasing the sensitivity of the experiment can be achieved by:

(a) increasing the error variance
(b) randomization
(c) increasing the variance due to the dependent variable
* (d) use of the precision control technique
(e) decreasing the variance due to the independent variable

7. Which of the following is true when matching by holding variables constant?

(a) it decreases the sensitivity of the experiment
* (b) it limits generalizability
(c) it is useful only for human studies
(d) it creates an inability to randomly assign subjects

8. Which of the following is <u>not</u> true of the technique of matching by building the extraneous variable into the design?

(a) it controls for the influence of the extraneous variable
(b) it uses the extraneous variables as independent variables
* (c) it identifies the interaction between levels of the extraneous variable
(d) it identifies the influence due to the extraneous variable

9. A disadvantage of matching by holding variables constant is:

(a) internal validity
(b) the inability to randomly assign subjects to conditions
* (c) a lack of external generalizability
(d) an increase in error variance

10. Matching by __________ takes a potential contaminating variable and changes it into an independent variable.

(a) precision control
(b) frequency control
* (c) building the extraneous variable into the design
(d) yoked control
(e) equating subjects

11. A problem with the precision control technique is:

(a) the difficulty in knowing which variable to match
(b) the difficulty of matching individuals
(c) the difficulty of finding matched subjects
(d) the difficulty of obtaining adequate measures of the variables to be matched
* (e) all of the above

12. The precision control technique has a number of disadvantages associated with its use. Which of the following is not a disadvantage?

(a) difficulty in knowing which variables to match
* (b) the matched variables do not influence the dependent variable differentially
(c) the more variables there are to match, the more difficult it is to match subjects
(d) some variables are difficult to match in individuals
(e) matching limits the generality of the results of the study

13. Matching by _________ attempts to match subjects in terms of an overall distribution of a selected variable or variables.

(a) yoked control
(b) precision control
* (c) frequency control
(d) building the extraneous variable into the design
(e) holding variables constant

14. The frequency distribution control technique matches subjects by:

(a) comparing subjects in terms of frequency of particular variables
(b) equating subjects on two variables
(c) equating groups of variables in the distribution
* (d) equaling the overall distribution of the variable to be matched.

15. If, as an experimenter, you are interested in controlling for the possible influence of the temporal relationship between an event and a response, which matching technique should you consider using?

(a) matching by building the extraneous variable into the research design
(b) matching by holding variables constant
* (c) matching by yoked control
(d) matching by equating subjects

16. With the precision control technique, the investigator matches subjects in the various treatment groups on a case-by-case basis for each of the selected extraneous variables. Which of the following is not a disadvantage of this approach?

(a) it is difficult to know which are the most important variables to match
(b) some variables are very difficult to match
(c) the difficulty of finding matched subjects increases disproportionately as the number of variables increases
* (d) it increases the sensitivity of the study

17. Which technique is used to control for sequencing effects?

(a) randomization
(b) precision control matching
* (c) counterbalancing
(d) frequency distribution control
(e) yoked control

18. Order effects can be attributed to:

(a) practice effects
(b) learning
(c) time of testing
(d) familiarity with the experimental situation
* (e) all of the above

19. The __________ counterbalancing technique controls for sequencing effects by the administration of the treatment to subjects in one stated order and then in the reverse order.

(a) randomized
(b) complete
(c) incomplete
* (d) intrasubject
(e) intersubject

20. The ABBA technique refers to:

* (a) intrasubject counterbalancing
(b) complete counterbalancing
(c) incomplete counterbalancing
(d) randomized counterbalancing
(e) none of the above

21. To control for nonlinear order effects one must use the:

(a) ABBA technique
(b) BAAB technique
* (c) ABBA and BAAB technique
(d) ABC technique

22. When carry over effects are nonlinear, they can be controlled by:

(a) randomized counterbalancing
(b) complete counterbalancing
(c) incomplete counterbalancing
(d) intrasubject counterbalancing
* (e) none of the above

23. The incomplete counterbalancing approach to intragroup counterbalancing requires that

(a) every possible sequence of the various treatment conditions must be enumerated and a different group of subjects take each of the enumerated sequences
(b) each subject take the treatment condition first in one order and then in the reverse order
* (c) the sequences enumerated be equal in number to the number of levels of the independent variable when the number of levels of the independent variable is an even number
(d) none of the above

24. Which technique used to control for demand characteristics requires that neither the experimenter nor the subject be aware of the treatment condition administered to the subject?

* (a) double blind placebo model
(b) deception
(c) disguised experiment
(d) independent assessment of the dependent variable

25. One method of controlling experimenter expectancy error allows the investigator to know the hypothesis but is blind as to which treatment condition the subject is in. This is referred to as

(a) the partial blind technique
(b) the double blind technique
(c) automaton
* (d) the blind technique

26. The method of controlling for experimenter expectancy error which keeps the experimenter ignorant of the condition the subject is in through as many stages of the study as possible is referred to as the

* (a) partial blind technique
  (b) automation technique
  (c) blind technique
  (d) double blind technique

27. Which of the following is used to create constancy of subject perceptions?

  (a) automation
  (b) double blind placebo
  (c) deception
  (d) disguising the experiment
* (e) b and c

28. Experimenter effects can be minimized by including techniques such as:

* (a) partial blind technique
  (b) deception
  (c) disguising the experiment
  (d) obtaining an independent measure of the dependent variable

29. The only method for control of unknown variables is:

* (a) randomization
  (b) counterbalancing
  (c) frequency distribution control
  (d) precision control

30. Kerlinger has suggested that matching is only useful if the variables on which subjects are matched correlated more than ___________ with the dependent variable.

  (a) .3 - .4
* (b) .5 - .6
  (c) .6 - .7
  (d) .7 - .8

31. The major disadvantage of the _________ technique of matching is that combinations of variables may be mismatched in various groups:

  (a) matching by holding variables constant
  (b) counterbalancing
* (c) frequency distribution control
  (d) ABBA

32. When every member of a population has an equal probability of being included in a sample, the sample is

(a) equivalent
* (b) random
(c) adequate
(d) stratified

33. When manipulations in an experiment appear identical to all subjects and the experimenter does not know which group is which, this is the approach.

* (a) double blind
(b) deception
(c) disguised
(d) automated

34. Sacrifice groups are an example of the use of:

* (a) concurrent verbal reports
(b) retrospective verbal reports
(c) postexperimental inquiry
(d) concurrent probing

35. Concurrent probing requires subjects to:

(a) report their perceptions as soon as the experiment is over
(b) report their perceptions before the beginning of the trial
* (c) report their perceptions at the end of each trial
(d) report their perceptions as they are performing the experimental task

36. The best means for controlling recording errors is to use:

(a) well trained observers
(b) multiple observers
(c) observers that are blind to the experimental conditions
* (d) mechanical or electronic devices

37. The experimenter attributes effects can be minimized if one controls for:

(a) deception
(b) subject effects
* (c) those attributes which correspond to the dependent variable
(d) sequential effects
(e) extraneous variables

38. The blind technique refers to:

(a) keeping the experimenter blind regarding the hypothesis of the experiment
(b) keeping the subject blind regarding the hypothesis of the experiment
(c) keeping the subjects blind with regard to the treatment conditions they are in
* (d) keeping the experimenter blind with regard to the treatment condition the subjects are in

39. At the present time most automated devices for conducting experiments

(a) are relatively inexpensive to purchase and program
* (b) do not totally remove the experimenter from the experimental environment
(c) can totally replace the experimenter in animal research
(d) show little promise for future research

40. When all subjects in an experiment perceive treatment conditions to be the same and when the experimenter does not know which group is which, the approach is being used:

* (a) double blind
(b) blind
(c) partial blind
(d) disguised

41. The double blind placebo model is infrequently used because:

(a) subjects cannot be randomly assigned to treatment conditions
(b) if any bias remains, it is not held constant across groups
(c) it does not completely eliminate the demand characteristics of the experiment
* (d) conditions can seldom be created so that they appear identical to all subjects

Fill In The Blank

1. A control technique that equates groups of subjects by ensuring every member has an equal chance of being assigned to any group is referred to as ____________.
(randomization)

2. A truly __________ sample is one that every member of the population has an equal probability of being included in it.
(random)

3. The random selection of subjects and the random assignment of subjects to treatment conditions are assumed to result in random distribution of all __________ __________ .
(extraneous variables)

4. __________ is the control technique used for controlling unknown sources of variation.
(randomization)

5. Randomization is generally considered to be the best means for attaining __________ __________ .
(internal validity)

6. __________ uses any of a variety of techniques for equating subjects on one or more variables.
(matching)

7. __________ control is a matching technique in which each subject is matched with another subject on selected variables whereas __________ control matches groups of subjects by equating the overall distribution of the chosen variable.
(precision; frequency distribution)

8. The __________ technique involves equating subjects on a case-by-case basis.
(precision control)

9. __________matching differs from __________ matching in that __________ corrects for a great number of subjects being lost because they cannot be matched perfectly.
(Frequency distribution; precision control; frequency distribution)

10. The yoked control matching technique is one that is employed to control for the possible influence of the __________ relationship between an event and a response.
(temporal)

11. __________ effects occur when performance is one treatment condition is partially dependent upon the conditions which precede it.
(sequencing)

12. Counterbalancing is the technique which is used to control for __________ effects.
(sequencing)

13. If Allen Funt were to carry out some of his Candid Camera routines as experimental studies, they would be termed _________ experiments because the subjects would be unaware that they were involved in an experiment.
(disguised)

14. At the present time the _________ technique is probably the best procedure for controlling for experimenter expectancies.
(blind)

15. Automation is a technique proposed to control for __________ bias.
(experimenter)

16. Carry over effects are a type of __________ effect.
(sequential)

17. The most basic control technique is __________.
(randomization)

18. __________ refers to the type of experiment wherein the subject is misled as to the true purpose of the experiment.
(Deception)

19. The two categories of methods that can be used to gain insight into subjects' perceptions of the experiment are the _________ verbal report where the subject recalls aspects of the experiment after completion and the __________ verbal report where the subject's report of the experiment is obtained during the experiment.
(retrospective;concurrent)

20. In cases where the blind technique cannot be used, it may be possible to keep the experimenter ignorant of the condition the subject is in for a portion of the study in order to reduce experimenter expectancy error. This is referred to as the __________ __________ technique.
(partial blind)

21. __________ of the experimental procedures, such as giving instruction and collecting data, attempts to eliminate investigator-subject interaction in order to reduce experimenter expectancy error.
(automation)

True or False

1. To provide for maximum control of extraneous variables, one ideally should randomly select subjects from the entire sample.
(False)

2. Random selection from a population is not the crucial element for providing control, whereas random assignment of the subjects to treatment conditions is essential.
(True)

3. Randomization allows for the equal probability that any variable will be assigned to any treatment group.
(True)

4. Random assignment eliminates sampling bias.
(False)

5. It is almost always possible to randomly select subjects from a given population.
(False)

6. Random selection is the crucial element for providing control in an experiment.
(False)

7. Randomization will always eliminate the chances of creating a biased distribution.
(False)

8. Randomization is the technique used for controlling unknown sources of variation.
(True)

9. Disadvantages of the matching technique include problems with restricting the available sample size and generalizing the results.
(True)

10. Matching by yoked control is recommended if one is interested in the differences produced by the various levels of the extraneous variable or in the interaction between the levels of the extraneous variable and other independent variables.
(False)

11. The frequency distribution control approach is one of the techniques commonly used to accomplish matching by equating subjects.
(True)

12. Dr. X used only males as subjects in his study because he thought females would confound the independent/dependent variable relationship. Dr. X controlled for the effect of this variable by building it into the design.
(False)

13. The classic executive monkey study, in which the temporal sequencing of administering shocks was equated across treatment groups is an example of yoked-control matching.
(True)

14. Order effects arise from the sequence of the treatment conditions that are administered to subjects.
(True)

15. An order effect is a sequencing effect that occurs when performance in one treatment condition affects performance in another treatment condition.
(False)

16. Sequencing effects, which can occur when the investigator constructs an experiment in which all subjects serve in each of several experimental conditions, may be controlled for with counterbalancing techniques.
(True)

17. The ABBA technique controls for nonlinear sequencing effects.
(False)

18. Counterbalancing techniques are not widely used.
(True)

19. An experimenter wishes to show that the list #2 is easier to learn than list #1. He gives subjects list #1 first, then list #2. List #2 is learned faster than list #1. The experimenter's conclusions may be invalid because he has not counterbalanced for a possible order effect.
(True)

20. The "think aloud" technique requires subjects to verbalize their thoughts at the end of the experiment.
(False)

21. Matching by yoked control is a method to reduce error variance by controlling for a temporal effect.
(True)

22. A disguised experiment is a method used to control for experimenter effects.
(False)

23. To use the method of deception to control for subject effects, a procedure must be established so that the independent variable as well as the dependent variable can be administered without telling subjects that they are in an experiment.
(False)

24. Of the several methods that can be used to gain insight into subjects' perceptions of the experiment, some consider the think-aloud technique to be the most effective because it does not require the subject to recall information.
(True)

25. To determine whether differential subject perceptions are created as a result of experimental procedures, it is necessary to use a technique such as the retrospective or concurrent verbal report.
(True)

Chapters 5-8

Integrative Questions

Answer questions 1 through 8 using the following information.

Dr. D. ran an experiment to study the effect of drug use on memory. Subjects were randomly assigned to one of two groups, defined by administration (group one) or non-administration (group two) of THC (active ingredient in marijuana). A list of thirty 3-letter words and a list of thirty 8-letter words were learned in succession, with a five minute free-recall period following the learning of each list. All subjects receive both lists, but the order of presentation of the two lists is counterbalanced across groups. In group one, two 3-letter and two 8-letter words are correctly recalled. In group two, fifteen 3-letter and ten 8-letter words are correctly recalled.

1. What is the dependent variable?

   (a) number of words presented per list
   * (b) number of words recalled per list
   (c) number of letters in words
   (d) number of minutes provided for free-recall

2. What is the between-subjects factor?

   * (a) drug administration
   (b) length of words in list
   (c) counterbalancing order
   (d) there is no between-subjects factor

3. How was the factor of drug administration manipulated

   (a) instructional manipulation
   * (b) event manipulation
   (c) individual difference manipulation
   (d) none of the above

4. What is the within-subjects factor?

   (a) drug administration
   * (b) length of words in list
   (c) counterbalancing order
   (d) there is no within-subjects factor

5. How was the factor word length varied?

   (a) presence versus absence technique
   (b) amount of a variable technique
 * (c) type of a variable technique
   (d) none of the above

6. There is a main effect of

   (a) marijuana
   (b) word list
 * (c) both marijuana and word list
   (d) neither marijuana nor word list

7. There is an interaction, showing that memory is better for short than for long words under normal conditions, and this difference in retention for short and for long words is accentuated by the use of marijuana.

   (a) true
 * (b) false, this is not what the interaction shows
   (c) false, there is no interaction only a main effect
   (d) false, there is no interaction but two main effects

Answer questions 15-19 based on the following information.

Dr. Edvale runs an experiment to study the effect of drug use on memory. Subjects are randomly assigned to one of two groups, defined by administration (group one) or non-administration (group two) of THC. Two different lists of words, list A having concrete words and list B abstract words, are learned in succession with a recall test following the learning of each list. All subjects receive both lists. To control for order effects, group 1 receives list A then list B, and group 2 receives the opposite order. Results (mean number of words correctly recalled out of a possible 50) are the following:

	Group One	Group Two
List A	30	50
List B	40	40

8. What type of design was used in the above example?

   (a) factorial between subjects
   (b) factorial within subjects
 * (c) factorial between-within subjects or mixed model design
   (d) factorial counterbalanced

9. What is the between subjects factor?

* (a) drug administration
  (b) type of word
  (c) counterbalancing order
  (d) there is no between subjects factor

10. What is the within subjects factor?

  (a) drug administration
* (b) type of word
  (c) counterbalancing order
  (d) there is no within subjects factor

11. There is a main effect of

* (a) drug
  (b) type of word
  (c) both drug and type of word
  (d) there are no main effects

12. There is an interaction, showing that concrete and abstract words are learned equally as well under normal conditions, but that retention is affected by drug use more for abstract than for concrete words.

  (a) true
* (b) false, this is not what the interaction shows
  (c) false, there is no interaction, only a main effect of type of word
  (d) false, there is no interaction, only a main effect of THC

Answer questions 13-17 based on the following information.

> You want to study the effect of alcohol on reasoning. You vary alcohol using the presence versus absence technique, and employ three different types of problems (math, verbal, spatial). Alcohol is used as a between subjects factor. Type of problem is a within subjects factor. You record the time taken to solve the problems. In the alcohol condition, it takes 6 minutes to do a math problem, 18 for verbal, and 12 for spatial. In the placebo condition, it takes 2 minutes for math problems, 5 for verbal and 3 for spatial.

13. Given the above information, it would be necessary to

* (a) randomly assign subjects to groups
  (b) randomly assign type of problem for each subject
  (c) counterbalance to avoid carry-over effects of alcohol
  (d) all of the above

14. This design is a

(a) 1 x 2 factorial
(b) 2 x 2 factorial
(c) 3 x 3 factorial
* (d) none of the above

15. There are __________ different conditions.

(a) two
(b) four
* (c) six
(d) nine

16. There is a main effect of

(a) alcohol
(b) type of problem
* (c) both drug and type of problem
(d) neither variable

17. There is an interaction, showing that reasoning involves more time for verbal, than for spatial, than for math problems under normal conditions, and this difference in reasoning time is accentuated by the use of alcohol.

* (a) true
(b) false, this is not what the interaction shows
(c) false, there is no interaction, only one main effect
(d) false, there is no interaction, but two main effects

Answer Questions 18 & 19 based on the following information.

In an experiment on the effects of word length on retention, subjects are first given 20 five letter words to learn, and then 20 eight letter words to learn.

18. The above experiment illustrates a

* (a) within subjects design
(b) between subjects design
(c) factorial design
(d) mixed model design

19. There is a possible confound in the above experiment which could be controlled for by having a control group.

(a) true
* (b) false

Answer Questions 20 & 21 based on the following information.

In order to study the effect of alcohol consumption on driving ability, Dr. Alky had one group of subjects drink 3 ounces of straight gin, and another group of subjects drink 3 ounces of liquid that tasted like gin, and then tested the performance of the two groups on a driving simulation task.

20. The method of generating variation used in Dr. Alky's experiment is

(a) the amount of variable technique
(b) the type of variable technique
* (c) the presence versus absence technique
(d) a standard agreed upon technique

21. The method of variation used by Dr. Alky is that which should be used when one wants to make an in-depth study of the effect of a given variable.

(a) true
* (b) false

22. The manipulation of the independent variable in Dr. Alky's study would be classified as

* (a) event manipulation
(b) instructional manipulation
(c) individual difference manipulation
(d) intentional manipulation

Answer questions 23-27 based on the following information.

The effect of stress on performance is studied. Twenty Ss are randomly selected for the study. All are told they will be tested for their creativity. They are given an object, and told to discover 15 unusual uses for it. Ten of the Ss are told they will receive a 50 volt shock at some time 60 sec after the beginning of the experiment. The other 10 Ss are just told they have 3 minutes to do the task.

23. This is a __________ design.

* (a) between subjects
(b) within subjects
(c) factorial
(d) none of the above

24. The method used to establish variation in the independent variable is

* (a) instructional manipulation
(b) individual difference manipulation
(c) event manipulation
(d) none of the above

25. The dependent variable would be

(a) amount of shock received
(b) number of objects given
(c) time given to discover unusual uses
* (d) number of unusual uses discovered

26. It would probably be a good idea to

* (a) match subjects prior to the experiment
(b) counterbalance unusual uses for the object
(c) counterbalance the order of shock and no shock condition
(d) hold constant the number of unusual uses actually discovered

27. What technique was used to control for subject effects?

(a) counterbalancing
(b) matching
* (c) deception
(d) verbal reports

CHAPTER 9

Experimental Research Design

Multiple Choice

1. Ten subjects state that they have a headache at 2:00 p.m. and are given aspirin. At 5:00 p.m. they are asked if they have a headache. They all report they do not. The conclusion that aspirin relieves headache is based upon which type of research design?

* (a) One group before-after
(b) Factorial
(c) Before-after
(d) One-group after-only
(e) After only

2. The primary disadvantage of the one-group before-after design is:

(a) uncontrolled subject loss
(b) lack of accurate statistical techniques
* (c) lack of a comparison group
(d) the "non-equivalence" of before and after comparison

3. The one-group after-only design is faulty because:

(a) not enough experimental groups are used
(b) it is not amenable to statistical analysis
* (c) it does not provide a comparison group
(d) it does not provide posttest information

4. The one-group before-after design is only slightly better than the one-group after-only design because of the:

(a) possible influence of extraneous variables
(b) possible impact of rival hypotheses
(c) problems with internal validity
(d) absence of a control group
* (e) all of the above

5. A one-group before-after design is an improvement over the one-group after-only design in that it includes:

(a) randomization
* (b) a pretest
(c) a posttest
(d) a control group
(e) proper statistical analyses

6. The nonequivalent post-test only design is faulty because:

(a) it provides no comparison group
(b) it does not match on relevant variables
(c) it is not amenable to statistical analysis
* (d) the subjects are not randomly assigned

7. Which of the following are criteria needed for a good research design?

(a) control of extraneous variables
(b) design must adequately test the hypothesis
(c) generalizability
(d) external validity
* (e) they are all criteria

8. Which of the following is required of a good research design?

(a) The design must prove the research question
* (b) The design must allow internal validity
(c) The design must allow statistical significance
(d) The design must allow external validity

9. Which of the following is not a reason for pretesting subjects?

(a) increasing the sensitivity of the experiment by matching
(b) to insure that a ceiling effect does not exist
(c) to test for the effect of initial position
(d) to insure the initial comparability of the groups
* (e) to assess subject motivation

10. Which of the following is not one of the advantages of pretesting?

(a) increased sensitivity
(b) assessing the possibility of a ceiling effect
(c) assessing a subject's initial position on a trait
(d) assessing initial comparability
* (e) all are advantages

11. Pretesting a subject may:

(a) facilitate the experimental effect
(b) depress the experimental effect
(c) increase design sensitivity
* (d) all of the above

12. If different subjects are used in each experimental treatment condition of a study, then the design is labeled a:

(a) within subject design
(b) intrasubject design
(c) intersubject design
* (d) between subject design

13. A basic after only design was used in a drug dosage study, except that several levels (dosages) of the independent variable were tested. What type of design was used?

(a) Factorial Design
* (b) Randomized Subjects Design
(c) Correlated Groups Design
(d) After Only Design
(e) Before-After Design

14. The simple randomized subjects design uses:

(a) more than one independent variable
(b) only one level of the independent variable
(c) several levels of several independent variables
* (d) several levels of one independent variable
(e) none of the above

15. A ___________ design is one in which two or more independent variables are simultaneously studied to determine their effects on the dependent variable.

(a) simple randomized subjects
* (b) factorial
(c) before-after
(d) mixed model
(e) after only

16. A Factorial Design allows for what types of effects that an After Only design does not.

* (a) Interaction Effects
(b) Regression Effects
(c) History Effects
(d) Maturation Effects
(e) Main Effects

17. An interaction effect refers to the influence that:

* (a) one independent variable has on another independent variable
 (b) arises from the manipulation of the independent variable
 (c) the independent variable has on the dependent variable
 (d) occurs as a result of the interaction between the various levels of the independent variable

18. A 3x3 factorial design has __________ cells.

 (a) 3
 (b) 6
* (c) 9
 (d) unable to say from the information given

19. A 2x2 factorial design will have a maximum of __________ main effects.

 (a) 1
* (b) 2
 (c) 9
 (d) unable to say from the information given

20. One of the disadvantages of the within subjects design is:

* (a) the potential for sequencing effects
 (b) decreased sensitivity of the design
 (c) its failure to include randomization
 (d) none of the above

21. All of the following are examples of faulty research design except:

 (a) one-group after-only
 (b) one-group before-after
* (c) after-only
 (d) nonequivalent posttest-only

22. Which of the following is a difficulty associated with a factorial design?

 (a) it may require a large number of subjects
 (b) it is difficult to simultaneously manipulate the combination of independent variables in this design
 (c) it may be difficult to interpret higher order interactions
* (d) all of the above

23. With regard to factorial designs, which of the following is an advantage?

    (a) multiple hypothesis can be tested
    (b) one can build confounding variables into the design
    (c) one has the ability to study interactive effects of independent variables
    (d) it provides greater precision in assessing the independent variable
  * (e) all of the above

24. Which of the following is not true of the within-subjects design:

    (a) it may involve matching of subjects
  * (b) it typically requires many subjects
    (c) it is very sensitive to the manipulation of the independent variable
    (d) it can be confounded by sequencing effects

25. When using a within subjects design a more sensitive measure of the __________ variable(s) can be provided.

    (a) dependent
    (b) control
    (c) extraneous
  * (d) independent
    (e) randomized

26. A repeated measures or within subjects design does a poor job of controlling for:

    (a) sequencing effects
    (b) history variables
    (c) subject maturation
  * (d) all of the above

27. In a factorial design A2 B1 most likely denotes:

    (a) a significant interaction
    (b) two significant main effects
  * (c) a treatment cell
    (d) both a & b

28. The primary criterion for selection of a research design is:

    (a) whether it is amenable to statistical analysis
  * (b) whether it enables one to answer the research question
    (c) whether it can incorporate the proper control techniques
    (d) whether it can rule out rival hypotheses

29. The __________ design has as a disadvantage of the fact that it does not provide assurance of equality between the group's (no random assignment).

(a) Before After
(b) After Only
(c) Factorial
* (d) Non-equivalent Posttest only

30. The design in which two or more independent variables are simultaneously studied is called

* (a) factorial
(b) before-after
(c) analysis of variance
(d) none of the above

31. The after-only research design is one which:

(a) assesses the dependent variable only once
(b) comprises the basic components used in most designs
(c) compares treatment group to a control group
(d) can use either a between subjects or a within subjects paradigm
* (e) all of the above

32. The within-subjects after-only design:

(a) is a repeated measures design
(b) provides perfectly equated subjects
(c) has subjects "serve as their own control"
* (d) all of the above

33. The greatest disadvantage of the within-subjects design is:

* (a) a possible nonlinear sequencing effect
(b) that it requires subject matching
(c) the existence of linear sequencing effects
(d) that it requires more subjects than the between groups design
(e) none of the above

34. A factorial design based on a mixed model refers to a combination of a __________ design and a __________ design:

(a) factorial; simple randomized subjects
* (b) between subjects; within subjects
(c) factorial; between subjects
(d) simple randomized subjects; between subjects

35. The reason(s) for pretesting is (are):

(a) increased sensitivity
(b) to determine whether there is a ceiling effect
(c) to determine initial position of subjects
(d) b and c
* (e) all of the above

36. The before after research design differs from the one-group before-after design in that the former includes __________ and__________.

(a) pretesting; randomization
(b) pretesting; a control group
* (c) a control group; randomization
(d) multiple regression analysis
(e) counterbalancing
(f) all of the above

37. Statistical regression is controlled for in the before-after design by utilizing:

(a) individual pretesting
* (b) an equated control group
(c) multiple regression analysis
(d) counterbalancing
(e) all of the above

38. An improvement of the before-after research design over the one group before-after design is:

(a) proper statistical analysis
(b) adding of a posttest
(c) added control for mortality
* (d) added control for history and maturation
(e) adding of a pretest

39. Concerning the "One-Group Before-After" research design:

(a) there is no attempt to measure the improvement of performance in this design
(b) the design allows the researcher to control for the influence of confounding variables
* (c) there may be rival hypotheses which account for any change in performance
(d) internal validity is assured with this design

Fill in the blank

1. Smith and Jones divided students reporting depression into two groups. They tested one group, did nothing to the other and then compared their scores on the Beck Depression Inventory. This is an example of a __________ design.
(nonequivalent posttest-only)

2. Another term for generalizability is __________ validity.
(external)

3. When extraneous variables have been controlled a study is said to be __________ valid.
(internally)

4. If different subjects are used in each experimental treatment condition, the design is labeled a __________ design.
(between subjects)

5. Increased sensitivity of the experiment and evidence of change are reasons for __________ subjects.
(pretesting)

6. A main effect refers to the influence of one __________.
(independent variable)

7. An experiment in which two or more independent variables are studied simultaneously is called a __________.
(factorial design)

8. As a general rule, a factorial design should be limited to __________ independent variables.
(three)

9. A within-subjects after-only design is also called a __________ design.
(repeated measures)

10. A within subjects design typically requires __________ subjects than the between subjects design.
(fewer)

11. A factorial design based on a mixed model represents the combination of a __________ subjects design and a __________ subjects.
(between; within)

12. When two or more independent variables are being investigated at the same time, it is necessary to use a __________design.
(factorial)

13. In order to determine if an interaction effect exists, it is necessary to use a __________ design.
(factorial)

14. The primary criterion for selection of a research design is whether it will enable one to answer the __________.
(research question)

15. When one has a choice of a between or a within subjects design, the choice is frequently made in favor of the __________ subjects design.
(within)

16. A design in which subjects serve as their own controls is called a __________ design.
(repeated measures or within-subjects after-only)

17. The most important technique to control for unassessed group differences is ___________.
(randomization)

18. An experiment which combines within and between subjects designs is called a __________.
(mixed model)

19. Sequencing effects can sometimes be controlled by __________
(counterbalancing)

20. Pretesting can be used to __________ subjects and thereby increase the sensitivity of the experiment.
(match)

21. Good research designs consist of the _________ and the__________ design because they can eliminate the influence of extraneous variables.
(after-only; before-after)

22. The ___________ research design represents the prototype of most research designs.
(after only)

23. The greatest disadvantage of the within-subjects design is ___________ effects.
(sequencing)

<u>True or False</u>

1. As a general rule researchers should not commit to a particular statistical analysis until their data has been gathered.
(False)

2. The one-group after-only design is an efficient way to utilize a small subject population.
(false)

3. When it is feasible, matching groups on demographic variables is preferable to random assignment to groups.
(false)

4. In some cases, pretesting may confound results by sensitizing subjects to the nature of the experimental task.
(true)

5. The greatest disadvantage of the within subjects design is linear sequencing effects.
(false)

6. Subjects must be pretested to maximize the sensitivity of the experiment.
(false)

7. There are two basic types of true research designs: the before-after and the staggered posttest.
(false)

8. An experimenter who both matches and randomizes his subjects increases the sensitivity of the design.
(true)

9. The simple randomized subject design does not permit one to investigate several independent variables simultaneously.
(true)

10. A main effect refers to the influence of one independent variable.
(true)

11. A factorial design is a variation of a before-after design which uses several independent variables.
(false)

12. When different subjects are used in each experimental condition of a study, the design is labeled a between subjects design.
(true)

13. The simple randomized design considers one level of several independent variables.
(false)

14. An interaction effect occurs when the levels of variation of one independent variable differentially affect the dependent variable.
(false)

15. Use of randomly assigned control and experimental groups will control for regression effects in the before-after design.
(true)

16. When both the main effect and interaction are significant a researcher should interpret only the interaction.
(true)

17. In a factorial experiment a researcher can control a potentially confounding variable by building it into the design.
(true)

18. A difficulty with factorial designs is interpretation of higher order interactions.
(true)

19. The problem with the one-group after-only design is that it provides nothing to compare results with.
(true)

20. The simple randomized subjects design is an after-only type of design that includes only one independent variable.
(true)

21. A factorial design is required to determine interaction effects.
(true)

22. A mixed model refers to a design combining randomization of subjects with matching for important characteristics.
(false)

Chapters 6 - 9

Integrative Questions

Answer questions 1-7, based on the following information.

> Dr. Snooze looked at the effect of sleep deprivation on cognitive functioning. He ran three groups of subjects at 8:00 a.m. Group A had slept 8 hours the night before, Group B had slept 4 hours, and Group C not at all (this was manipulated by Dr. Snooze). All subjects performed two tasks: (1) sort a deck of cards, (2) solve a complicated maze. The time needed to complete each task was recorded.

1. What is the dependent variable?

   (a) the amount of time given to complete the tasks
   * (b) the amount of time taken to complete the tasks
   (c) the amount of time slept the night before
   (d) the time the experiment was run in the morning

2. What is (are) the between subjects factor(s)?

   * (a) the number of hours slept the night before
   (b) the type of task performed
   (c) both the number of hours slept the night before and the type of task performed.
   (d) none of the above

3. What is (are) the within subjects factor(s)?

   (a) the number of hours slept the night before
   * (b) the type of task performed
   (c) both the number of hours slept the night before and the type of task performed.
   (d) none of the above

4. Which variable should be controlled for through counterbalancing?

   (a) the number of hours slept the night before
   * (b) the type of task performed
   (c) both the number of hours slept the night before and the type of task performed
   (d) none of the above

5. Which variable should be controlled for through random assignment?

* (a) the number of hours slept the night before
(b) the type of task performed
(c) both the number of hours slept the night before and the type of task performed
(d) none of the above

6. If you matched subjects, what would be advisable to match on?

(a) previous experience with mazes
(b) knowledge of the organization of card decks
(c) normal television viewing habits
* (d) a and b

7. What is the design of the experiment?

(a) 2 x 1 within-subjects design
(b) 3 x 8 factorial design
* (c) 3 x 2 factorial design
(d) 8 x 4 between-subjects design

Chapter 10

Quasi-Experimental designs

Multiple Choice

1. What distinguishes a non-equivalent control group design from a before-after experimental design:

   * (a) the way subjects are assigned to groups
   (b) the number of subjects used
   (c) the number of hypotheses tested
   (d) the use or absence of pretesting

2. In which of the following settings would it be appropriate to use a quasi-experimental design?

   (a) Natural disasters
   (b) Child abuse
   (c) Planned interventions such as a persuasive communication designed to change behavior
   (d) An academic setting to test the effect of absences on grades
   * (e) all of the above

3. If one applies an experimental mode of analysis and interpretation to situations and the resulting data which do not meet the full requirements of experimental control, one has employed a:

   (a) correlational design
   * (b) quasi-experimental design
   (c) true experimental design
   (d) type of descriptive experimentation

4. Assume a researcher designates one class of children to be the experimental group and another class the control group. Both groups are given a pre- and posttest and the experimental group is given the treatment condition between pre- and posttesting. The researcher would be using a:

   (a) time series design
   (b) simulated before after design
   (c) multiple baseline design
   * (d) nonequivalent control group design

5. What should be the experimenters primary concern when using the nonequivalent control group design?

   (a) sample size
* (b) rival hypotheses
   (c) experimenter bias
   (d) choice of statistical test

6. Two groups in a quasi-experimental design were matched prior to the experiment. Following the experimental treatment the two groups differ significantly on the dependent measure. This could have resulted from:

   (a) selection-maturation effect
   (b) the experimental treatment
   (c) statistical regression to the mean
* (d) any of the above.

7. An experimenter has selected two groups for quasi-experimental design. The control group had a beer at Al's Pub & Pizza between pre and posttesting and performed quite poorly at posttest. This is an example of:

   (a) selection-maturation effect
   (b) statistical regression
* (c) local history effect
   (d) unequivalent groups

8. A researcher finds that the variability of his subject's scores has increased following the experimental manipulation. This has most likely resulted from:

* (a) selection-maturation effects
   (b) random chance
   (c) the experimental treatment
   (d) statistical regression

9. A researcher finds that his experimental group, who scored significantly lower than the control group at pretest, now scores significantly higher following the experimental treatment. This has most likely resulted from:

   (a) statistical regression
* (b) a crossover effect
   (c) a selection-maturation effect
   (d) discontinuity

10. The increasing treatment effect I outcome is a situation in which the control group reveals __________ from pretest to posttest but the experimental group starts at a higher level and shows __________.

(a) significant change; no change
(b) no change; significant negative change
(c) significant change; significant positive change
* (d) no change: significant positive change

11. The increasing treatment effect II is an outcome which is potentially confounded by __________ rival hypothesis.

(a) maturation
(b) history
* (c) statistical regression
(d) instrumentation
(e) subject bias

12. Which of the following rival hypotheses is eliminated by the cross over effect?

(a) Instrumentation
* (b) Selection-maturation
(c) History
(d) Mortality
(e) Subject bias

13. An experimental design in which the researcher examines the patterns of pre and post responses is called a:

(a) response analysis design
* (b) time-series design
(c) regression-discontinuity design
(d) none of the above

14. The major advantage of a multiple time-series design over an interrupted time series design is that it:

(a) establishes patterns for more than one behavior
(b) is more sensitive to subtle patterns of change
* (c) eliminates the history effect as an alternative hypothesis
(d) there is no advantage over the interrupted time-series

15. The interrupted time-series design is one that requires the investigator to take measurements __________ the treatment condition.

(a) before
(b) after
* (c) before and after
(d) during

16. If one takes a series of measurements before and after the introduction of some treatment condition one would have employed a:

(a) simulated before-after design
(b) reversal design
* (c) interrupted time-series design
(d) multiple baseline design

17. The effect of the treatment condition in the time series design is noted by:

(a) the return to baseline upon removal of treatment
* (b) the discontinuity in the recorded series of response measures
(c) the significant difference in the pre- versus posttest scores

18. The multiple time series design differs from the interrupted time series design because it eliminated the __________ effect.

* (a) history
(b) selection
(c) maturation
(d) statistical regression

19. The nonequivalent control group design is an example of a ____________ design.

(a) time series
* (b) before-after
(c) cohort
(d) none of the above

20. __________ is the primary rival hypothesis that is eliminated by the cross over effect.

* (a) selection-maturation
(b) history
(c) experimenter effects
(d) instrumentation

21. A rival hypothesis that exists in the increasing treatment effect I outcome is:

(a) general history effect
(b) instrumentation
* (c) local history effect
(d) statistical regression

22. A situation in which both the control and experimental groups show an increment in the dependent variable from pre to posttesting as a possible result of a selection-maturation bias is:

(a) increasing treatment effect I
(b) increasing treatment effect II
(c) cross over effect
* (d) increasing treatment and control groups

23. The __________ renders many rival hypothesis implausible,

* (a) cross over effect
(b) increasing treatment effect I
(c) increasing treatment and control groups
(d) increasing treatment effect 11

24. Although matching may control for the potential bias of the selection-maturation effect, it does not eliminate the rival hypothesis of __________ when using a quasi-experimental design.

(a) subject bias
(b) instrumentation
(c) statistical regression
(d) experimenter bias
* (e) all of the above

25. Quasi experimental designs should be used when:

(a) subjects cannot be randomly assigned to conditions
(b) it is not possible to control all extraneous variables
(c) it is not possible to directly manipulate the independent variable
* (d) all of the above

26. If the variability of scores for the experimental and control groups increases from pretesting to posttesting, this suggests the rival hypothesis of:

(a) statistical regression
* (b) selection-maturation
(c) history
(d) instrumentation
(e) mortality

Fill in the Blank

1. The essence of what is termed Quasi-Experimental Designs is the lack of complete __________.
(control)

2. The difference between a nonequivalent before-after design and an experimental before-after design is that groups are not assigned __________ to treatment conditions in the nonequivalent before-after design.
(randomly)

3. The one characteristic which most often distinguishes quasi-experimental designs from true experimental designs is the lack of __________ __________ in the quasi-experimental design.
(random assignment of subjects)

4. An increase in the variability of subject scores from pre to post testing most likely results from a __________.
(selection-maturation interaction)

5. In some studies the treatment and control groups are not equated by age. The most readily apparent confounding effect due to this fact is __________.
(maturation)

6. The __________ effect illustrates an outcome from a nonequivalent control group design in which most of the common rival hypotheses are rendered implausible.
(cross over)

7. The __________ effect refers to an experimental outcome in which the treatment group scores significantly lower than the control group at pretest time but significantly higher at posttest time.
(cross over)

8. Every month a man's weight is measured for one year (12 measurements). He then goes on a special diet to lose weight. After the diet is initiated the man measures his weight as before every month for a year. This is an example of a(n) ________ design to study the effects of the diet on weight.
(time series)

9. One way to check for the existence of a statistical regression artifact in extreme groups is__________ .
(multiple pretesting)

10. The __________ __________ __________ is a statistical procedure that determines whether the pattern of post response measures differs from the pattern of pre response measures.
(moving average model)

11. An experimenter has collected 20 pretest measures and is planning to collect at least that many following the treatment. He is most likely using a __________ design.
(time-series)

12. An experimenter has collected 20 pretest measures and is planning to collect at least that many following the treatment. He is doing this for both an experimental and control group. This is called a __________ design.
(multiple time-series)

13. Gallup County has been collecting crime statistics for each town for the last 10 years. The crime rate in Bilton has dropped for 5 consecutive years following the introduction of unmarked police cars. To test the hypothesis that the new cars are responsible the researcher looked at the crime rate patterns for the surrounding towns without unmarked cars. This is an example of a __________ design.
(multiple time-series)

14. A __________ effect may occur when one of the two groups of subjects are chosen in such a way that they are developing faster than the subjects in the other group.
(selection by maturation)

15. The interrupted time series differs from the multiple time-series in that it does not control for a(n) __________ effect.
(history)

16. The __________ __________is a statistical analysis used to analyze time series data.
(moving average model)

17. Statistical regression can be eliminated by a __________ effect.
(cross over)

True/False

1. It is possible to make causal inferences from quasi-experimental designs.
(true)

2. Although matching offers a possible control for the selection maturation effect in a nonequivalent control group design, it does not entirely exclude the possibility of a statistical regression effect.
(true)

3. Suppose that the experimental and control group in a nonequivalent control group design both increase in performance after a treatment, but that the experimental group increases at a greater rate. Because the control group also increases in performance the difference between the two groups cannot be due to a selection-maturation effect.
(false)

4. In a nonequivalent control group design random assignment of subjects to treatment groups leads to "nonequivalent" groups.
(false)

5. In a nonequivalent control group design subjects are randomly assigned to each group.
(false)

6. Use of matching techniques in the nonequivalent control group design will assure that subjects are totally equated.
(false)

7. The tendency for extreme scores to regress towards the mean is known as statistical compensation.
(false)

8. The mean of a group containing several scores in the extreme upper end of a distribution is likely to be lower on subsequent measurements.
(true)

9. A crossover effect is a type of interaction.
(true)

10. Cross over effects render most rival hypotheses implausible.
(true)

11. A general history effect is a rival hypothesis that exists in the increasing treatment effect outcome.
(false)

12. Measurements are taken before and after treatment in the interrupted time series design.
(true)

13. Multiple time-series designs compensate for the lack of a control group by increasing the number of pre and posttest assessments.
(false)

14. The chief difference between Interrupted and Multiple time-series designs is the length of time between pre and post testing.
(false)

Chapter 11

Single-Subject Research Techniques

<u>Multiple Choice</u>

1. In a single subject design, what serves the function of a control (comparison) group?

    (a) Posttreatment responses
    (b) The mean posttreatment response for a given population
    (c) The treatment condition itself
  * (d) Pretreatment responses
    (e) Conditioned responses

2. Which of the following favored single-subject designs:

  * (a) B.F. Skinner
    (b) Ronald Fisher
    (c) Eddie Fisher
    (d) Eysenck
    (e) all of the above

3. Another name or description for an A-B-A design is:

    (a) antecedent-Behavior-Altered design
  * (b) baseline-Treatment-Baseline design
    (c) treatment Discontinuity
    (d) multiple Baseline design

4. In the A-B-A design, the second A symbolizes:

    (a) baseline rate
    (b) treatment response stabilization
  * (c) withdrawal or reversal of treatment (return to baseline)
    (d) the treatment condition
    (e) the pretreatment rate

5. One problem with the A-B-A design is that it:

  * (a) terminates with baseline
    (b) provides no standard for comparison
    (c) has no control group
    (d) is not amendable to multiple subject application

6. Which of the following is not a problem of the A-B-A design:

    (a) it ends the study on a baseline
    (b) reversal to baseline does not occur with some behaviors
  * (c) it is difficult to implement with only one subject
    (d) all the above are problems of the A-B-A design.

7. From the standpoint of a therapist, the A-B-A design denies the benefits of treatment. This disadvantage could be overcome if the design were changed to a(n):

* (a) ABAB design
(b) AAB design
(c) changing criterion design
(d) multiple baseline design
(e) interaction design

8. What might facilitate the attainment of a reversal to baseline in an A-B-A design?

(a) multiple manipulation of the independent variable
(b) an especially potent treatment
(c) extended treatment sessions
* (d) short experimental periods

9. This design involves investigating the effects of two separate independent variables by analyzing the influence of each variable separately and in combination.

(a) multiple Baseline design
(b) changing criterion design
(c) ABA design
(d) time Series design
* (e) interaction design

10. In order for the multiple baseline to be effective in evaluating treatment effects, the target behaviors must be:

(a) correlated
* (b) independent
(c) interdependent
(d) extraneous
(e) generalizable

11. Multiple-baseline design can be applied to different:

(a) people
(b) situations
(c) behaviors
* (d) all of the above
(e) b and c but not a

12. Which of the following is not a recommendation for dealing with interdependence of behaviors in multiple-baseline designs:

(a) select behaviors empirically shown to be independent
(b) use four or more baselines
* (e) decrease error variance by using fewer subjects
(d) implement a reversal on one of the baseline behaviors
(e) all of the above are correct

13. The effectiveness of a multiple baseline design hinges on:

(a) a reversal of behavior to baseline level
(b) generalization of effects across conditions, behavior, or individuals
* (c) maintenance of nontreated behaviors at baseline
(d) a high degree of interdependence of behaviors

14. When using a multiple baseline design, an assessment of independence of behavior should occur _______ treatment.

(a) before
(b) during
(c) after
* (d) before and after

15. Which of the following is necessary when using a multiple baseline design?

* (a) selection of independent behaviors
(b) implement several treatments
(c) vary length of the baseline for each subject
(d) implement a reversal on one of the baseline behaviors

16. The design which has proven most useful in shaping behavior over a period of time is the:

* (a) changing-criterion design
(b) multiple-baseline design
(c) alternating-treatment design
(d) A-B-A design
(e) none has proven particularly useful for this purpose

17. Which of the following is false with regard to the changing criterion design?

(a) it requires a baseline
* (b) the criterion for performance changes at random
(c) the criterion for performance proceeds in a stepwise fashion
(d) The treatment phases may last for different lengths of time

18. An essential requirement of a changing criterion design is that it must manifest:

(a) return to initial baseline
(b) constant responses across different situations
(c) socially desirable behavior
* (d) successively improved or increased baseline rates
(e) statistical significance

19. Which of the following is true?

(a) A stable baseline is more difficult to attain with animals than humans.
(b) In some single subject research it is necessary to change more than one variable from phase to phase of the experiment.
* (c) Cyclic variation in single subject research can be remedied somewhat by extending the measurement period of each phase.
(d) Statistical analyses are unnecessary in single subject research.

20. The only single-subject design which allows the experimenter to alter more than one behavior at a time is the:

(a) A-B-A-B design
(b) alternating-treatment design
(c) multiple-baseline design
(d) changing-criterion design
* (e) none of the above

21. What is the most important issue to consider about a baseline?

(a) duration
(b) frequency
* (c) stability
(d) temporal equivalence

22. In most cases the degree of variability in the baseline in animal experiments is __________ in humans.

* (a) less than
(b) slightly greater than
(c) about the same as
(d) much greater than

23. In single subject designs how many variables can be changed when proceeding from one phase of the experiment to the next?

* (a) 1
(b) 2
(c) 3 at most
(d) as many as can reasonably be managed

24. Generally speaking, the length of phases in the baseline and treatment:

(a) should vary differentially according to type of treatment
(b) should vary differentially according to type of behavior
* (c) should be as equal as possible
(d) should vary differentially according to type of design

25. The two criteria which have typically been employed in single subject research consist of a(n) __________ criterion and a(n) __________ criterion.

(a) experimental; treatment
(b) baseline; treatment
(c) experimental; baseline
* (d) experimental; therapeutic

26. Social validation of a treatment effect is accomplished by either a __________ comparison method or by a __________ evaluation method.

(a) therapeutic; social
(b) experimental; subjective
(c) social; experimental
* (d) social; subjective

27. The ________ comparison method involves comparing the behavior of a client before and after treatment with his/her nondeviant peers.

(a) subjective
* (b) social
(c) experimental
(d) objective

28. The __________ evaluation method refers to assessing whether the treatment led to qualitative changes in how others view the subject.

* (a) subjective
(b) social
(c) objective
(d) therapeutic

29. Which of the following methods is a means of evaluating the therapeutic criterion of a treatment.

(a) social isolation
(b) statistical analysis
(c) reversal
* (d) subjective evaluation
(e) all of the above

30. Perhaps the greatest advantage of the single-subject design over the multi-subject design is:

(a) it lacks intrasubject variation differences
(b) its control over extraneous variables
* (c) it lacks intersubject variation differences
(d) it can rule out more rival hypotheses

31. All single subject research designs are one form of:

(a) an ex post factor design
* (b) a time series design
(c) factorial designs
(d) exchanging criterion designs
(e) ABA design

32. A time series design:

* (a) requires repeated dependent measures before and after the treatment condition
(b) requires repeated dependent measures only after the treatment condition
(c) requires repeated treatment conditions
(d) is a special case of a cross-sectional study
(e) is another name for a longitudinal study

33. The difference between an ABA withdrawal design and an ABA reversal design is that in the reversal design:

* (a) the treatment is shifted to another target
(b) the treatment is removed completely
(c) more than one level of the treatment can be used
(d) statistical analyses cannot be performed
(e) return to baseline is much easier to accomplish

34. Rival hypotheses in single-subject designs include:

(a) experimenter expectancies
(b) sequencing effects
(c) change produced by instructions
(d) history
* (e) all of the above

35. Single-subject designs are especially useful for:

(a) starting an investigation in a new area of inquiry
(b) examining individual differences
(c) establishing causality
* (d) a and b
(e) all of the above

36. The most critical component of the reversal or ABA design is the demonstration of:

* (a) a return to baseline when treatment conditions are withdrawn
(b) pre- versus post treatment differences
(c) a change in behavior when treatment conditions are instituted none of these
(d) none of these

<u>Fill in the Blank</u>

1. A single-subject study requires some sort of _________ design.
(time series)

2. A subject's behavior prior to treatment intervention is called the __________.
(baseline)

3. The most basic single subject research design is the ________ design.
(ABA)

4. For situations in which the changes in target behavior are "irreversible" the best design would be a __________ design.
(Multiple baseline)

5. One of the chief difficulties of the multiple-baseline design is __________.
(interdependence of behaviors)

6. In the ________ design, baseline data are collected on several different behaviors for the same individual.
(multiple baseline)

7. Reversal of behavior back to its pretreatment level is of crucial importance in the __________ design.
(ABA)

8. In order for the multiple-baseline-design to be effective, there must not be __________ of behaviors.
(interdependence)

9. A design in which the subject must meet increasingly difficult criterion is called a _________ _________ design.
(changing criterion)

10. The __________ __________ design is useful for studies that involve the shaping of behavior.
(changing criterion)

11. The _________ __________ design is an improvement over the A-B-A design in that it does not involve the removal of the treatment condition.
(multiple baseline)

12. The recording of target behaviors as they occur naturally is _________.
(baseline)

13. Instructions and experimenter expectancies are two examples of _________ __________.
(rival hypotheses)

14. __________ of phases during the baseline and treatment should be as equal as possible.
(Length)

15. In single-subject research, the number of variables that can be changed from one phase of the experiment to the next is __________.
(one)

16. The most important issue to consider about the baseline is __________.
(stability)

17. The clinical significance or value of the treatment effect for the subject is referred to as the __________ criterion.
(therapeutic)

18. Social validation, social comparison, and subjective evaluation are all methods for establishing the __________ of a treatment.
(therapeutic criterion)

19. One of the advantages of the single-subject design over the multisubject design is the elimination of intersubject __________.
(variability or difference)

True or False

1. A single-subject design and a case study are conducted the same way.
(False)

2. Single-subject designs are a recent innovation which has greatly expanded the field of study for experimental psychology.
(False)

3. Several treatments must be implemented in a multiple baseline design.
(True)

4. Brief experimental periods may facilitate the attainment of a reversal to baseline in the ABA design
(True)

5. Single subject designs require the use of some form of a time series design.
(True)

6. The changing-criterion design is a design that is most useful for shaping behavior.
(True)

7. One disadvantage of the single-subject design is the inability to look at interactions.
(False)

8. To effectively evaluate treatment effects in a multiple baseline design it is important that the dependent variables be independent of each other.
(True)

9. Counterbalancing is critical in a multiple-baseline design.
(False)

10. In the changing-criterion design the increases in criterion difficulty should always be as small as possible to enhance compliance by the subject.
(False)

11. Statistical analysis of single-subject designs is impossible due to the absence of between group variability.
(False)

12. Generally speaking, the experimental phase should be considered longer than the baseline.
(False)

13. The most important issue to consider about the baseline is stability.
(True)

14. In animal research there is usually greater variability in the baseline than in human research.
(False)

15. In single subject research, the maximum number of variables that can be changed from one phase of the experiment to the next is three.
(False)

16. The social comparison method refers to the comparison of the behavior of the client before and after treatment with the behavior of his/her nondeviant peers.
(True)

17. Social validation involves determining whether the treatment led to differences in how others view the subject.
(False)

18. Elimination of intrasubject variation is the main advantage of single subject designs.
(False)

19. The therapeutic criterion of a treatment is more difficult to demonstrate than is the experimental criterion.
(True)

Chapter 10-11

Integrative Questions

Answer questions 1-5 based on the following information.

A researcher wanted to study the effect of a tutoring program on improving quiz scores. Three students served as subjects. During baseline, students received no tutoring, and the scores or quizzes given throughout the week were recorded. Starting on Day 10, the first student (Roy) began receiving tutoring whenever he obtained a D or F grade on a quiz. Baseline conditions were maintained for the other two students (Fred and Ginger). On Day 15, Fred began his tutoring contingency, whereas Ginger's tutoring contingency began on Day 20.

1. The design used in the above example is a ______ design.

   (a) changing criterion
   * (b) multiple baseline
   (c) alternating treatments
   (d) interaction design

2. This type of design can also be considered as three

   * (a) separate AB designs
   (b) separate ABA designs
   (c) separate ABAB designs
   (d) none of the above

3. This type of design can be applied to different

   (a) people
   (b) situations
   (c) behaviors
   * (d) all of the above

4. Suppose that not only Roy, but Fred and Ginger as well suddenly started getting better scores on quizzes on Day 11. What could one assume about the behaviors of the subjects?

   (a) that they are varied
   (b) that they are controlled
   (c) that they are independent
   * (d) that they are interdependent

5. If Fred and Ginger also started obtaining better scores on Day 11, It could be concluded that the tutoring program was indeed effective.

    (a) True
* (b) False

Answer Questions 6-8 based on the following information.

The below illustrates a nonequivalent control group design, since the assignment of subjects to groups was not random:

Group A: pretest - treatment - posttest measurement
Group B: pretest - no treatment - posttest measurement

6. How would one estimate the initial equivalence of the two groups with respect to the dependent variable?

* (a) compare pretest measurement of the two groups
    (b) compare posttest measurement of the two groups
    (c) compare both the pretest measurements of both groups and the posttest measurement of both groups
    (d) compare the difference between pre- and posttest scores in the experimental group to the difference between pre- and posttest scores in the control group

7. How would one determine whether or not the treatment had an effect?

    (a) compare pretest measurements of the two groups
    (b) compare posttest measurements of the two groups
    (c) compare both the pretest measurements of both groups and the posttest measurements of both groups
* (d) compare the difference between pre- and posttest scores in the experimental group to the difference between pre- and posttest scores in the control group

8. What effect(s), aside from that of the treatment, could account for a difference between the two groups at the end of the experiment?

    (a) selection-maturation effect
    (b) local history effect
    (c) statistical regression to the mean
* (d) any of the above

Chapter 12

Data Collection and Hypothesis Testing

1. Long-Evans, Sprague-Dawley and Wistar are:

   (a) research colleagues of B. F. Skinner
   (b) authors of the APA's Guidelines for Data Collection
   * (c) types of rats
   (d) a and b
   (e) all of the above

2. The two most common subject types in psychological research are:

   (a) The albino rat and the pigeon
   (b) The college sophomore and children
   (c) The albino rat and children
   * (d) The albino rat and the college sophomore

3. Human subjects are generally selected:

   (a) randomly
   * (b) on the basis of convenience and availability
   (c) according to APA standards
   (d) from a representative sample of the population

4. If subjects can't be randomly selected, the best solution is:

   (a) choose another organism for subjects
   * (b) randomly assign subjects to treatments
   (c) match subjects on the relevant variables
   (d) postpone the study until more subjects are available

5. Ideally, random selection of subjects is preferred, but practically:

   (a) random assignment is preferred to random selection
   (b) random selection can only be accomplished in the laboratory
   (c) this cannot be done, because so many people want to participate
   (d) random observation is conducted in field studies
   * (e) random assignment is the only type of randomization possible

6. What usually determines the number of subjects used by most researchers?

* (a) the number of subjects used by other investigators within the area
  (b) the size of the subject pool
  (c) sequential analyses
  (d) the amount of time available

7. Researchers most often decide on sample size for a study based on:

  (a) statistical formulas estimating the power of their research design.
* (b) research precedents
  (c) available financial resources
  (d) the number of subjects immediately available

8. Which of the following is not one of the data collection considerations mentioned by the author:

  (a) subjects
  (b) sample size
  (c) apparatus
  (d) instructions
* (e) hypothesis testing

9. When subjects fail to show up for an experiment the best procedure is probably to:

  (a) estimate their performance from group averages.
* (b) randomly assign replacement subjects in their place.
  (c) consider it a random attrition and do nothing
  (d) offer greater incentives for participation

10. Which of the following is not a function of apparatus?

  (a) facilitate the administration of the independent variable
  (b) allow for the systematic presentation of independent variables
  (c) allow for the systematic recording and measurement of dependent variables
* (d) enables one to separate the effects of different levels of the independent variable

11. According to one rule of thumb, when using an analysis of variance design with several levels of the independent variable, approximately how many subjects per cell should be used?

* (a) 15
(b) 5
(c) 35
(d) 32
(e) 125

12. Which is not a purpose served by the instructions of an experiment?

(a) definition of the task
* (b) classification of the variables
(c) motivation of subjects
(d) direction of attention

13. The primary rule to follow in the data collection stage of an experiment is:

* (a) adhere to the prepared procedure
(b) maintain equivalence of subjects
(c) hold extraneous variables constant
(d) test different independent variables until the most appropriate one is found

14. Which of the following is not a function of the post-experimental interview?

(a) ethical function
(b) educational function
* (c) pretest function
(d) subject satisfaction function

15. A pilot study:

(a) seems necessary only when past results have been contradictory
(b) requires a large number of subjects
(c) if conclusive, precludes the necessity of a larger scale study
(d) assesses the need for a certain study to be conducted
* (e) assesses the validity and sensitivity of the independent and dependent variables

16. A pilot study is:

(a) usually necessary only in more complex designs
(b) ill advised when the research design requires deception
* (c) considered a pretest of the experiment
(d) all of the above

17. The primary rule in data collection is:

* (a) adhere as closely as possible to the outlined procedure
(b) make sure that subjects are debriefed in full
(c) choose the correct measurement devices
(d) not to introduce experimental contaminants
(e) replicate the results of a pilot study

18. Research has shown that subjects perceive psychological experiments to be most deficient in their_________ value.

(a) scientific
(b) ethical
(c) satisfaction
* (d) educational

19. The purpose of the postexperimental interview is to:

(a) allow the subject to comment on the experiment
(b) gather information regarding the subjects' thinking or strategy during the experiment
(c) contribute to the subjects' satisfaction with their role in the experiment.
(d) probe the subjects' perceptions of the experimental requirements
* (e) all of the above

20. What should be the main determinant guiding the selection of an organism for the study?

(a) availability
* (b) research problem
(c) precedent
(d) ethics

21. Which of the following is the proper sequence to be followed when conducting a psychological study?

(a) debriefing, subject selection, data collection, hypothesis testing
(b) subject selection, data collection, hypothesis testing, debriefing
(c) hypothesis testing, subject selection, data collection, debriefing
* (d) subject selection, data collection, debriefing, hypothesis testing

22. The two most common types of subjects in psychological research are:

* (a) college sophomores and rats
(b) college sophomores and pigeons
(c) pigeons and rats
(d) rats and children

23. Pilot studies allow one to determine if:

(a) instructions are clear
(b) the independent variable has the intended effect
(c) the dependent variable is sensitive to the effect of the independent variable
* (d) all of the above

<u>Fill in the Blank</u>

1. A researcher is conducting a study in the local grade school. Only 29 of the 136 parents contacted agreed to let their children participate. This introduces the potential confound of __________.
(selection bias)

2. The memory drum, relay rack and snap leads have mostly been replaced by the __________.
(microcomputer)

3. The memory drum and microcomputer are both types of experimental __________.
(apparatus)

4. A _________ represents a run-through trial of the experiment with a small number of subjects.
(pilot study)

5. An experiment conducted prior to the actual collection of data is called a __________
(pilot study)

6. In order to return subjects to their pre-experimental state, the experimenter must conduct a _______________.
(debriefing or-post experimental interview)

7. Studies have indicated that many subjects believe that psychological experiments are deficient in their __________ value.
(educational)

8. The standard laboratory animal for research is the __________
(white rat)

9. Instructions to subjects must be _________, ________and ________, but not too complex.
(clear, unambiguous,specific)

True or False

1. If a study is well designed it makes little difference what type or species of subject is used.
(False)

2. Sidowski and Lockard have suggested that the albino rats used for any one study actually represent a homogeneous subset and are probably not representative of the overall albino rat population.
(True)

3. One of the major advantages of nonhuman subjects is that scheduling does not have to be considered.
(False)

4. Psychology experiments are typically perceived by subjects as lacking educational value.
(True)

5. Debriefings are often used for methodological reasons.
(True)

6. Studies indicate that most subjects believe that psychological experiments are of great educational value.
(False)

7. A researcher can never be sure that the differences observed from an experiment are real and not due to chance.
(True)

8. Precedence usually determines the number of subjects to be used in a study.
(True)

9. The main determinant guiding the selection of an organism should be the research problem.
(True)

10. A pilot study is necessary only when past results have been contradictory.
(False)

CHAPTER 13

Hypothesis Testing

Multiple Choice

1. The hypothesis that is always tested is the null hypothesis because

   (a) this is the hypothesis that conforms to our predicted relationship
* (b) it is impossible to test the scientific hypothesis
   (c) our interest typically lies in the null hypothesis
   (d) the null hypothesis can only be confirmed and not rejected

2. When the null hypothesis is tested we are actually testing

* (a) whether we are dealing with one or two populations
   (b) whether the scientific hypothesis is true
   (c) the experimental hypothesis
   (d) if the mean in the population is the same as the sample mean

3. If the null hypothesis is rejected you are

   (a) providing indirect evidence for the scientific hypothesis
   (b) stating that two populations exist
   (c) providing support for the scientific hypothesis
* (d) supporting all of the above

4. The mean is

* (a) the arithmetic average of a group of scores
   (b) a measure of the variability of a group of scores
   (c) a measure of the range of scores
   (d) used to indicate the most frequently made score

5. If you have conducted an experiment investigating the effect of caffeine or no caffeine on fatigue and found that the caffeine group could stay awake an average of 11 hours before getting tired whereas the no caffeine group became fatigued after staying awake only 9 hours you would know

   (a) that caffeine cause a reduction in fatigue
   (b) caffeine is a powerful drug effecting sleep
* (c) that the central tendency of the caffeine group was 11 hours whereas the central tendency of the noncaffeine group was 9 hours
   (d) caffeine has a real effect on perceived fatigue

6. The most frequently used measure of variability is

(a) range
(b) average deviation
* (c) standard deviation
(d) interquartile range

7. If group A has a standard deviation of 5 and group B has a standard deviation of 10, we know that

* (a) the scores of group B are more variable than those of group A
(b) group A scores are significantly different from those of group B
(c) group B scores are twice as large as those of group A
(d) group A scores has a mean of 2.5 and group B scores has a mean of 5

8. If group A has a mean of 50 and a standard deviation of 10 and group B has a mean of 45 and a standard deviation of 15, the most likely outcome is that

(a) a significant difference exists between the means of the two groups
* (b) a nonsignificant difference exists between the means of the two groups
(c) the scientific hypothesis of a group difference would be supported
(d) the null hypothesis would be rejected

9. If group A has a mean of 50 and a standard deviation of 10 and group B has a mean of 40 and a standard deviation of 5, from only this only thing you can conclude is that

(a) the null hypothesis can be rejected
(b) the null hypothesis can be accepted
(c) group A is significantly different from group B
* (d) the two groups may differ significantly because they do not overlap extensively

10. Statistical tests allow us to

(a) reject the null hypothesis with complete certainty
(b) accept the null hypothesis
* (c) estimate the magnitude of difference between group means that can be expected by chance
(d) test the scientific hypothesis

11. The statistical test used in a given study is

(a) the same as that used by other investigators
* (b) dictated by the study design
(c) a function of whether animals or humans are being investigated
(d) dictated by the research question
(e) must be determined by a statistician

12. Twenty rats are randomly assigned to a drug or no drug group and tested on speed with which they can solve a choice discrimination problem. What statistical test should be used to determine if the drug effects speed of problem solving.

* (a) independent samples t-test
(b) one-way analysis of variance
(c) correlated t-test
(d) repeated measures analysis of variance

13. If you are comparing the difference between two group means to the average variability within each of these two groups, you have computed

* (a) an independent samples t-test
(b) a one-way analysis of variance
(c) a correlated t-test
(d) a repeated measures analysis of variance

14. As the variability between groups increases relative to the variability within groups

(a) the t-test becomes smaller
(b) chances of rejecting the null hypothesis decrease
(c) the probability of attaining significance decreases
* (d) the probability of rejecting the null hypothesis increases

15. Thirty rats were randomly assigned to received 10, 20, or 30 mg of cocaine to determine its effect on speed with which they could traverse a maze. What type of statistical test should be used to analyze the data.

(a) an independent samples t-test
* (b) a one-way analysis of variance
(c) a correlated t-test
(d) a repeated measures analysis of variance

16. If you have measured the overall variation of the scores obtained from all subjects you have a measure of

    (a) between-groups variation
    (b) within-groups variation
    (c) variance within
*   (d) total variation

17. If you combine variation between groups and the variation within groups, you would have

    (a) a t-ratio
*   (b) total variation
    (c) analysis of variance
    (d) a means square analysis
    (e) a parametric statistical test

18. The between groups variance is actually a measure of

    (a) the effect produced by the independent variable
    (b) chance variability
    (c) the variability of the subjects within a single group
    (d) the scientific hypothesis
*   (e) both a and b

19. The ratio of the between to the within-groups variance is

    (a) a t-test
    (b) a correlated t-ratio
*   (c) an F-ratio
    (d) total variation

20. If the F-ratio is equal to 1

    (a) there is no treatment effect
    (b) the between-groups variance is just chance variability
    (c) the within-groups variance is just chance variability
    (d) you could not reject the null hypothesis
*   (e) all of the above

21. If the between-groups variance is 10 times larger than the within-groups variance we know that the F-ratio

*   (a) is at least 10
    (b) is at least 20
    (c) is less than 1
    (d) degrees of freedom are also 10

22. A research obtains a significance level of .25 for his experimental results. This indicates that:

* (a) the results are quite possibly due to chance alone
(b) the results are significant by the standards most commonly used to judge experimental results
(c) the differences observed are likely to occur by chance 2.5 times out of 100
(d) a and c
(e) b and c

23. A researcher tells you that the results from his last study obtained a significance level of .07 and thus indicated acceptance of the null hypothesis. You doubt this because:

(a) .07 would usually be considered a significant result
* (b) it is very difficult to obtain acceptance of the null
(c) a significance level of .07 is impossible
(d) a significance level of .07 does not allow one to test the null hypothesis
(e) you know this researcher and he wouldn't know a null hypothesis from a rat's nose

24. Changing the significance level from .01 to .001 would most likely:

* (a) increase the probability of a Type II error
(b) decrease the probability of a Type II error
(c) increase the probability of a Type I error
(d) have no effect on Type I or Type II errors
(e) b and c

25. In statistical computations, if the obtained difference between the scores of various groups has not reached the specified significance level, then the experiment:

(a) accepts the null hypothesis
(b) rejects the null hypothesis
* (c) fails to reject the null hypothesis
(d) accepts the scientific hypothesis

26. A type I error refers to:

* (a) accepting the scientific hypothesis as true when it is false
(b) rejecting the scientific hypothesis when it is true
(c) failing to reject the null hypothesis when the scientific hypothesis is true
(d) accepting the null hypothesis when it is false

27. In general, which is true?

(a) Accepting the null is more serious than rejecting the scientific hypothesis
* (b) Committing a Type I error is considered more serious than committing a Type II error
(c) Type II error is usually of no consequence in psychological research
(d) Increasing Type I error increases Type II error also
(e) Type II error is controlled directly by the selection of an arbitrary significance level

28. A type II error refers to:

(a) accepting the scientific hypothesis when it is false
(b) rejecting the scientific hypothesis when it is true
* (c) failure to reject the null hypothesis when it is false
(d) accepting the null hypothesis when it is false

29. In general, the risk of committing a type I error ___________ as the risk of committing a type II error ____________, and the risk of committing a type II error ___________ as the risk of committing a type I error __________.

(a) increases; increases; decreases; decreases
(b) decreases;increases;increases;increases
(c) decreases; decreases; increases; increases
* (d) increases; decreases; increases; decreases

30. In most instances, which type of error is most detrimental?

* (a) type I
(b) type II
(c) type III
(d) they are equally detrimental

31. How can the possibility of a type II error be minimized?

(a) lower the significance level
* (b) raise the significance level
(c) increase the number of subjects
(d) use a conservative statistical technique

32. If an investigator finds no significant relationship between the independent and dependent variable then:

(a) the scientific hypothesis is accepted
* (b) the null hypothesis is not rejected
(c) the null hypothesis is rejected
(d) the null hypothesis is accepted

33. If a difference is significant at the .01 level, chance could account for this difference ________ percent of the time.

* (a) 1
(b) 10
(c) 90
(d) 99

34. A researcher obtains a significant level of .25 for his experimental results. This indicates that

* (a) the results are quite plausibly due to chance alone
(b) the results are significant by the standards most commonly used to judge experimental results
(c) the differences observed are likely to occur by chance 2.5 times out of 100
(d) a and c

35. The .05 level of significance states that the observed difference is so large that it could have occurred by chance only _________ percent of the time.

* (a) 5
(b) 25
(c) 50
(d) 95
(e) 99

Fill in the Blank

1. __________ is a decision making process.
(hypothesis testing)

2. The most frequently used measure of variability in psychological research is __________.
(standard deviation)

3. The statistical test used to analyze data from two different groups of subjects is the __________.
(t-test)

4. __________ would be used to statistically analyze data collected from more than two groups of subjects.
(analysis of variance)

5. Between groups variance is a combination of the __________ and __________.
(treatment effect; chance variability)

6. Within groups variance is a measure of_____________.
(chance variability)

7. __________ is a combination of between and within groups variation.
(total variation)

8. The __________ is the ratio of between to within groups variance.
(F-ratio)

9. A ___________ error refers to accepting the scientific hypothesis as true, when it is actually false.
(Type 1)

10. In most instances, a Type __________ error is most detrimental.
(I)

11. If an investigator finds a significant relationship between the independent and dependent variables, then the ___________ hypothesis is accepted.
(scientific)

12. Any statistical test represents a test of the _________ hypothesis
(null)

13. A (n) __________ __________ is a statement of the probability that an observed difference is a chance difference.
(significance level)

14. A Type _________ error refers to rejecting the scientific hypothesis when it is true.
(II)

15. One step an experimenter can take to minimize Type II errors is to __________ the probability of rejecting the null hypothesis when it is in fact false.
(increase)

16. A researcher obtains a significance level of .25 for his experimental results. He should probably ________ the null hypothesis.
(fail to reject)

17. If the obtained difference between an experimental and control group does not reach the specified significance level the experimenter __________ the null hypothesis.
(fails to reject)

18. In order to correctly reject the null hypothesis 95% of the time a researcher must set a significance level of ________
(.05)

True or False

1. If the null hypothesis is rejected you are dealing with one population.
(False)

2. The mean is a measure of central tendency.
(True)

3. A small standard deviation indicates that the scores cluster closely about the mean.
(True)

4. The type of statistical analysis to use in analyzing the data is dictated by the study design.
(True)

5. Analysis of variance is used to test the difference between the means of only two groups.
(False)

6. Within-groups variance is actually a measure of two different sources of variability.
(False)

7. Within-groups variability is equal to chance variability
(True)

6. The F-ratio is the ratio of between to within-groups variance.
(True)

9. If the F-ratio is greater than 1 you know that a treatment effect does not exist.
(False)

10. In order to support the scientific hypothesis, one must accept the null hypothesis.
(False)

11. A significance level is a statement of the probability that an observed difference is a chance difference.
(True)

12. If obtained differences do not reach the significance level, then the experimenter accepts the null hypothesis.
(False)

13. Even though the null hypothesis can never be truly accepted, practical concerns demand that we sometimes act as though the null hypothesis were true.
(True)

14. A type I error is directly controlled by the researchers sample size and procedures.
(False)

15. Increasing the probability of Type II error would most likely be accompanied by a decrease in the probability of Type I error.
(True)

16. If we falsely reject the null hypothesis, than we have made a Type II error.
(False)

17. In most cases, a Type I error is considered to be worse.
(True)

18. The level of significance which is set for an experiment may be partially determined by the relative seriousness of committing a Type II versus a Type I error.
(True)

Chapter 14

External Validity

<u>Multiple Choice</u>

1. Generalization refers to:

   (a) internal validity
   * (b) external validity
   (c) convergent validity
   (d) divergent validity
   (e) face validity

2. External validity refers to the extent to which the results of an experiment can be generalized to and across different types of:

   (a) settings
   (b) times
   (c) persons
   * (d) all of the above

3. The threats to the external validity of an experiment fall into the category of:

   (a) time validity
   (b) ecological validity
   * (c) population validity
   (d) all of the above

4. Which of the following is not listed in the book as a potential threat to external validity:

   (a) population validity
   * (b) economic validity
   (c) ecological validity
   (d) time validity
   (e) all were mentioned

5. A researcher finds that many students, when given the opportunity, will cheat on a classroom exam. When given the same opportunity during job application, however, they do not cheat. The classroom results thus lack:

   (a) population validity
   * (b) ecological validity
   (c) reliability
   (d) time validity
   (e) all of the above

6. The experimentally accessible population is ___________ representative of the target population.

* (a) rarely
(b) always
(c) never
(d) usually

7. External validity refers to a _____________ by ___________ interaction.

(a) subject: setting
(b) subject; time
* (c) selection; treatment
(d) time; treatment
(e) time; selection

8. If the results of a laboratory experiment that requires a specific setting can be generalized to other settings, then the experiment possesses ___________ validity.

(a) concurrent
* (b) ecological
(e) population
(d) predictive
(e) time

9. The multiple treatment interference phenomenon can threaten validity.

* (a) ecological
(b) time
(c) population
(d) internal

10. The suggestion that each subject participate in only one experiment attempts to control:

(a) time validity
(b) the Hawthorne effect
(c) the experimenter effect
* (d) multiple-treatment interference
(e) none of the above

11. Multiple Treatment Interference represents a type of __________ effect.

* (a) sequencing
(b) experimental
(c) time span
(d) pretesting
(e) Hawthorne

12. Tom knew he was in an experiment, therefore, he acted much less naturally than he normally would have. This is an example of the:

(a) Experimenter effect
* (b) Hawthorne effect
(c) Time span effect
(d) Pretesting effect
(e) Sequencing effect

13. A researcher has been observing the effects of the university's recent anti-littering campaign by recording student littering in the university square. He has gathered his observations from a 7th story window. He has probably eliminated the problem of:

* (a) the Hawthorne effect
(b) ecological validity
(c) population validity
(d) economic validity
(e) b and c

14. Some research has found this effect not to be robust. Other research, however, has suggested that failure to find this effect was due to differential motivational states between volunteer subjects. Which effect is being referred to?

(a) Experimenter
(b) Time Span
(c) Hawthorne
* (d) Pretesting
(e) History

15. In psychological research subjects are most often chosen by:

(a) random selection
* (b) availability
(c) random assignment
(d) representation
(e) generalizability

16. A young man, when told by his mother, at home, to be quiet does so. The same young man, when told by his teacher, in school, to be quiet does not. External validity is not met here because of:

(a) population invalidity
* (b) ecological invalidity
(c) descriptive invalidity
(d) face invalidity
(e) convergent invalidity

17. The __________ effect refers to the fact that one's performance in an experiment is affected by knowledge of the fact that one is in an experiment.

(a) pretesting
(b) experimenter
(c) multiple treatment interference
* (d) Hawthorne
(e) disruption

18. A ___________ variation represents a variation which appears regularly over time in units of the population such as might exist with the number of automobile accidents.

* (a) seasonal
(b) random time
(c) personalogical
(d) cyclical
(e) temporal

19. A __________ variation represents a variation that occurs within people or organisms.

(a) fixed time
(b) variable time
(c) cyclical
* (d) personalogical
(e) random time

20. __________ variation refers to variation in the characteristics of individuals over time.

(a) Cyclical
* (b) Personalogical
(c) Seasonal
(d) Individual
(e) Variable time

21. Initially, the primary objective of a study emphasizes ___________ validity.

(a) ecological
(b) population
* (c) internal
(d) external
(e) time

22. If the experimental treatment effect does not interact with __________, then one can generalize the treatment effect.

(a) persons
(b) time
(c) settings
* (d) all of the above

23. An experimenter finds, at the end of the semester, that she is unable to replicate the results she obtained two months earlier. This illustrates a problem with the study's:

(a) ecological validity
(b) target population
(c) ergonomic validity
* (d) temporal validity
(e) c and d

24. Increasing external validity is likely to:

(a) increase the study's generalizability
(b) decrease the study's internal validity
(c) decrease the number of subjects necessary
* (d) a and b
(e) all of the above

25. A study in which the most effective treatment depends upon the type of person being considered:

(a) is demonstrating an ordinal interaction
(b) is demonstrating a disordinal interaction
(c) has limited generalizability
(d) a and c
* (e) b and c

26. Approximately _________ of studies listed in the literature use college students as subjects:

(a) 35%
(b) 50%
* (c) 75%
(d) 90%

27. A(n) __________ interaction is one where the rank order of the treatment effects remains the same across persons, settings, and times.

(a) sequencing
* (b) ordinal
(c) rank order
(d) disordinal

28. A(n) __________ interaction is one where the rank order of treatments changes across persons, settings, or times.

* (a) disordinal
(b) treatment x subject
(c) ordinal
(d) sequencing

29. __________ interactions do not limit generalizability of results where as __________ interactions do.

(a) disordinal; treatment
(b) ordinal; treatment
* (c) ordinal; disordinal
(d) ordinal; sequencing
(e) disordinal; ordinal

30. In __________ interactions the differences between persons, groups, or times must be statistically significant.

(a) treatment x subject
(b) ordinal
(c) sequencing
* (d) disordinal

31. The sample of subjects available to the experimenter is known as the:

* (a) experimentally accessible population
(b) target population
(c) representative population
(d) random sample

32. Fixed time variation is a type of __________ variation.

* (a) cyclical
(b) personalogical
(c) representative population
(d) random sample

33. According to Campbell and Stanley, if a __________ interaction exists the experiment is externally invalid.

(a) sequencing
(b) ordinal
(c) disordinal
* (d) selection x treatment

34. When considering the environment of the experiment in reference to external validity one is referring to:

(a) population validity
(b) ordinal interactions
(c) disordinal interactions
* (d) ecological validity

35. Environmental conditions of the experiment refer to:

(a) the physical setting of the experiment
(b) time of day the experiment is conducted
(c) type of experimenter
* (d) all of the above

Fill in the Blanks

1. Although it is readily seen that it is difficult to ________ select subjects from a target population, it is also difficult to __________ select subjects from the experimentally __________ population.
(randomly; randomly; accessible)

2. The ___________ __________ population refers to the subjects on which most experiments are conducted.
(experimentally accessible)

3. Generalizability from the study sample to the larger population of interest is called ________.
(population validity)

4. In order to generalize from the research sample to the target population a researcher must first be able to generalize from the research sample to the ___________.
(experimentally accessible sample)

5. The __________ population is the larger population to whom the results of the study are generalized.
(target)

6. The ability to generalize from the study sample to a larger population is referred to as __________ validity.
(population)

7. _________ validity refers to the ability to generalize the results of a study across settings.
(Ecological)

8. The Multiple Treatment Interference Phenomenon refers to a type of __________ effect.
(sequencing)

9. The effect that participation in one treatment condition has on participation in a second treatment condition is referred to as the __________ __________ __________ phenomenon.
(multiple treatment interference)

10. The __________ is similar to the Hawthorne effect.
(novelty or disruption effect)

11. The stress that most students feel at finals would be an example of ___________ variation.
(seasonal or fixed-time)

12. Fixed-time variation is a type of _________ variation.
(seasonal)

13. Personalogical variation refers to variation in the characteristics of _________ over time.
(individuals)

14. Regular variation that occurs within people or other individuals is referred to as __________ variation.
(cyclical)

15. The degree to which the results of an experiment can be generalized across time is referred to as __________ validity.
(time)

16. A(n) __________ variation is one that appears regularly over time in parts of the population.
(seasonal)

17. The tightly controlled and artificial setting of the laboratory would seem to threaten _________.
(external validity)

18. A researcher's first consideration should be the ____________ validity of the study.
(internal)

19. The problem of generalization from a sample to a population can be described as a(n) __________ by __________ interaction.
(selection, treatment)

20. Treatment A has a greater effect on population X than treatment B. The same holds for population Y, that is, treatment A has a greater effect than treatment B. Even though a subject by treatment interaction may occur, this type of interaction would be a(n) ________ interaction.
(ordinal)

21. __________ interaction limits the generalizability of results because rank orders of treatment effects are inconsistent across samples.
(Disordinal)

22. If a researcher wonders whether the treatment results for any given sample generalize from Los Angeles to New York, she is faced with a question of __________ validity.
(ecological)

23. If subjects are required to participate in more than one treatment condition, the threat of __________ __________ interference exists.
(multiple treatment)

<u>True or False</u>

1. The long-range goal of any experiment is to understand the basic underlying laws of behavior.
(True)

2. External validity asks the question of whether our research results are generalizable to other populations.
(True)

3. The experimentally accessible sample is identical to the sample used in the study.
(False)

4. There is increasing suspicion that the subjects in research studies are not representative of humans in general.
(True)

5. One way to increase generalizability of results is to make the experimental treatment as novel as possible in order to hold the subjects' attention.
(False)

6. Increasing the external validity of a study often decreases the study's internal validity.
(True)

7. An experimenter who does not seek to generalize the results of his study to the real world does not need to be concerned with internal validity.
(False)

8. A fixed-time variation is a variation that occurs after specific events, the timing of whose occurrence is not known.
(False)

9. A cyclical variation is a form of seasonal variation.
(True)

10. An ordinal interaction is one in which the rank order of the treatments changes across persons, settings, or times.
(False)

11. The Hawthorne effect refers to the fact that one's performance in an experiment is affected by knowledge that one is in an experiment.
(True)

12. Ecological validity exists to the extent that the treatment effect is independent of the experimental setting.
(True)

13. Multiple-treatment interference occurs within experiments but not between experiments.
(False)

14. A novelty or disruption effect refers to the influence produced by the knowledge that one is in an experiment.
(False)

15. When external validity is increased, internal validity usually decreases.
(True)

16. A disordinal interaction may limit a study's generalizability.
(True)

17. A phenomenon which can not be generalized to the target population is most likely an artifact of chance.
(False)

18. When internal validity is increased, external validity usually increases.
(False)

19. An ordinal interaction is one in which the rank order of the treatment effects remains the same across persons, settings, and times.
(True)

Notes

Notes